Yacky dar moy bewty!

Yacky dar moy bewty!

A Phrasebook for the Regions of Britain (with Irish Supplement)

by Sam Llewellyn

Elm Tree Books · London

First published in Great Britain 1985
by Hamish Hamilton Ltd/Elm Tree Books Ltd
Garden House 57-59 Long Acre London WC2E 9JZ

Cartoons by Nigel Paige

Llewellyn, Sam
Yacky dar moy bewty : a phrasebook for the regions of Britain (with Irish supplement)
1. English language — Dialects
I. Title
427 PE1711

ISBN 0-241-11390-3

Typeset by Pioneer, East Sussex.
Printed in Great Britain by Richard Clay
The Chaucer Press, Bungay, Suffolk.

CONTENTS

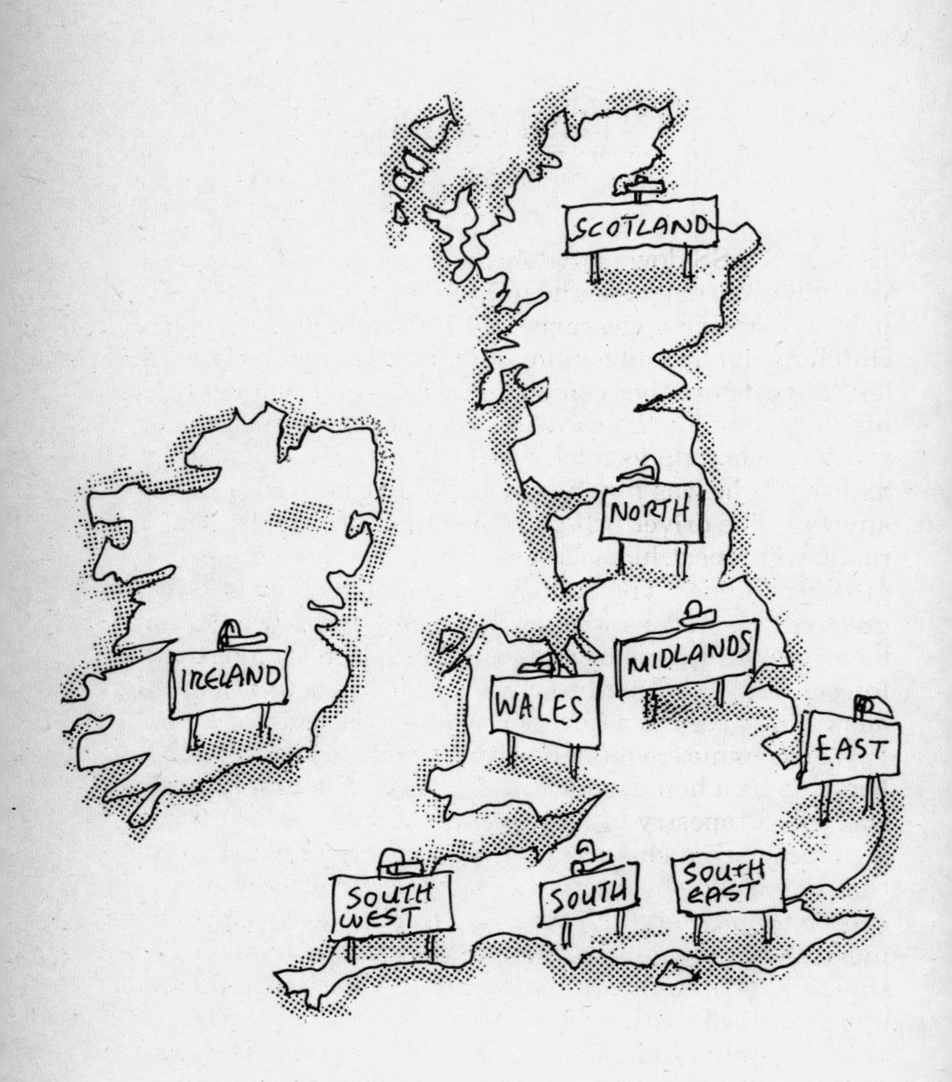
SCOTLAND
IRELAND
NORTH
MIDLANDS
WALES
EAST
SOUTH WEST
SOUTH
SOUTH EAST

INTRODUCTION

IF YOU PASS down any lane in the country this summer, you will eventually see the following sight. A person of pale and sweaty appearance will be sitting in a clean car, clutching a map and looking haggard. Immediately on his left, his wife or other companion will be snarling evilly. On his right, outside the car window, a person of rustic mien will be explaining in thick dialect that the map is wrong and that if he was him he wouldn't have started from here anyway. The driver will gape uncomprehendingly. The rustic will repeat himself some five times, his patience growing thinner. The holidaymaker (for such he is) will greet the repetitions with an increasingly sickly grin, until he drives off in despair and loses himself in the bogs and forests. Later that night he will be hit in a public house for answering "yes" to a question whose right answer is "no".

Wait a minute, you may say. Nowadays the English language is a homogenous mass. Once, of course, Britain was a rich tapestry of fascinating dialects, each with its own fascinating character. What a pity (you may continue) that universal education, the National Health Service, speech therapy and the spread of Sunday newspapers have made such a diversity a thing of the past. Having delivered this funeral oration you may retire to your lair to dream of apple-cheeked rustics cheering the Squire.

But happily, funeral orations are premature. The regions of Britain are pullulating with vigour, the differences between them deepening with every day that passes. In certain cases — one thinks immediately of Liverpool, Greater London and parts of Northern Ireland — they are beginning to look like republican city states with governments and languages of their own. More than ever before, ignorance of the linguistic conventions of the place you are in can land you in an amazing amount of trouble. This falls into two main categories.

1. What did he say?
and 2. Why did he do *that*?

1. What did he say?
As we have seen this mainly afflicts travellers for pleasure, e.g. when asking directions in navigational black spots such as Caersws or Bodmin. Symptoms are: complete inability to grasp the sense of a Regional Utterance, complicated by a feeling that if you ask the Regional Utterer to repeat himself one more time the Regional Utterer will probably blog you one in the ear.

2. Why did he do that?
Often, travellers find themselves in receipt of e.g. a broken jaw in a public house in Glasgow, for no reason they can perceive. Regional sensibilities are often both tender and markedly different from Standard English ones, and so are the meanings of words (c.f. "pony" in Gloucestershire, Newmarket Races and South London).

The object of this book is to provide (as far as possible) answers to both these questions, by giving in phrasebook form a key to the language and attitudes of the main regions of Britain and Ireland.

How to Use this Book
For the purposes of this book, Great Britain and Ireland have been divided into nine main language regions (see map). According to good phrasebook practice, each region has an introduction to give the traveller an idea of appropriate attitude, suitable clothing and equipment. There follows a pronunciation note. Next come lists of phrases for use in specific situations; and finally, there are entries that deal either with important sub-regions, or topics of extreme significance in the regional life.

To use this book, simply turn to the section dealing with the region in which you find yourself at a linguistic loss, turn to the appropriate subject heading, and start reading. You will find yourself drawn immediately into close *rapport* with the language and attitudes of your regional interlocutor. In time you will start to pick up fragments of speech over and above the ones in this book. And one day, you may become fluent!

Linguistic Note

Purists will say that the choice of nine regions does not reflect the true number of dialects that exists in Great Britain and Ireland. There are more like nine thousand, they will say. And rightly. This is not, however, a dialect dictionary, but a phrasebook. Extensive testing has shown that the regional languages used are, unless otherwise stated, comprehensible *throughout* the region in question, much as the lingua franca of the Mediterranean coasts united seafarers in the late Middle Ages.

Pronunciation

While there are several excellent phonetic alphabets in use, they are all a good deal too boring for phrasebook purposes, so we have used the standard alphabet and adjusted regional spellings to express the regional sounds as closely as possible when pronounced by a speaker of standard English.

Grammar

Though regional grammar is held by those in the know to be as deeply idiosyncratic as regional vocabulary, the casual linguist is unlikely to notice any grammar in the regions.

SOUTH WEST

Introduction

A HUNDRED AND fifty years ago, the voyage to the West Country was a comfortless affair of stage coaches, flea-ridden beds and encounters with bandits. Nowadays, it is a comfortless affair of traffic jams, nylon sheets and encounters with bandits. While the content has changed, the form remains more or less the same. This goes for the language too.

South-westerly parts of England do not need to be hidden in the Pictish twilight to possess their own idiosyncrasies. In Somerset, for instance, the sight of figures wearing cricket jerseys seven years overdue the wash and driving Austin A70 pickups at a rapid zigzag along bottomless lanes is a sure sign of the Cider culture. Similarly in Devon we see the blue-veined pallor of the Cream Tea fanatic and in Bath the limp wrist and perpetually skewed neck of the Neo-Palladian.

South West is as nowhere else in England the region of the Incomer. The caravan sites run a rich gamut of pastel hues and foreign accents. The villages have largely been taken over by nostalgic bank managers from Purley. The aboriginal inhabitants have reacted in two ways, both of interest to the linguist. One is to standardise their speech until any idiot can understand it. The other, favoured by the more Pictish, is a direct emulation of their Iberian forefathers. Faced with invasion, this lot historically fled to hills, isles and other spots that nobody else wanted. They now speak in a code so obscure that they frequently fail to understand even fellow Picts. The chief manifestation of this is, of course, the recent revival of the long-dead Cornish language.

Pronunciation Note
In Cornwall, speak as far as possible without moving the lips, projecting the voice at the inside of the forehead and grinning menacingly the while. In Devon, speak with great slowness and try when saying the letter "r" to emulate an accelerating Massey-Ferguson tractor. In Somerset, go for a high yipping delivery, close in spirit to the seam bowling of Joel Garner, alias Big Bird.

Travel

Ear yoe!	*Excuse me!*
Ace?	*Yes?*
Can ee dellus the rawed vor Penzarnce?	*Please tell me the way to Penzance.*
Whoart?	*I beg your pardon?*
PENZARNCE!	*PENZANCE!*
Thic be Larnsen, nart Penzarnce.	*But you are in Launceston.*
Ace.	*Precisely.*
A! You'll be awantin the Mooderaway.	*Proceed via the M5.*

Wheer's the Mooderaway?	*How do I reach the M5?*
Juz vore the rawed.	*It is ten miles away.*
Durn leaft at the Jurch . . .	*Left at the church . . .*
raight at the wold howse . . .	*right at the old house . . .*
down the combe . . .	*along the valley . . .*
and orver the burge.	*and across the bridge.*
Zixty yaard leater, you're on the bype arse.	*Sixty yards, and you're on the bypass.*
Carnt miss ut.	*The skeletons of your predecessors litter the verges.*
Arl raight, me luvver?	*Have you understood, sir?*
Ace. Tar.	*Yes. Thank you.*
Rawed do look a bit muxy, edna?	*The lane looks rather muddy, doesn't it?*
He aren't muxy, er's puxy.	*Muddy? Hip deep, cock.*
Give I a 'and if I stogs.	*Can you push me out if I get stuck?*
Oh, ah. Weal, I be off omelong.	*I'll be off home, then.*
Blast! I be stogged!	*Oh dear! I'm stuck! Help!*
Whoart?	*Sorry, I can't hear you.*
I be zinking!	*I'm going down!*
Whoart?	*I believe I am out of earshot.*
Zodomy! Stogged and ztuck fast!	*Curses! Irretrievably stuck!*
Vunny lart, them vrom up gundry.	*Odd folk, the inhabitants of continental England.*

Eating and Sleeping

I be zdarved.	*I am hungry.*
That thur be a caff vore the rawed.	*There is a restaurant down the road.*
Two crame tay, my anzums?	*Two cream teas, is it?*

Rarether!	*Yes, indeed.*
I do worship a crame tay.	*I much enjoy cream teas.*
Breave laddow crame you gart.	*You have plenty of cream.*
Parse the jarmpo, meate.	*Could you pass the jampot?*
This yur?	*This one?*
No, that thur.	*No, that one.*
I be vull.	*I have had enough.*
Whoart? Yu mimsey-pimsey, yu!	*Really? Are you sure?*
Waydress! Two more splits, a pig tart and tiddies . . .	*Waitress! Two more of those excellent buns, a pork pie with potatoes . . .*
and hell us more tay.	*and pour us some more tea.*
Whale! That were a prarperjarb.	*Phew! What a fine tea.*

Have you a bade, may purty mead?	*Have you overnight accommodation, miss?*
Zingle (durble), pleaze.	*Single (double), please.*
I can't abide nylarn zheets.	*Let us inspect the linen.*
Would'ee jeck springs, may purty mead?	*Could you test the springs, miss?*
Jonnick!	*Excellent.*
Anglish or candinendle brefiss?	*English or continental breakfast?*
Can't abide that vurrin cauch.	*I do not like continental breakfast.*
Marnin, may purty mead!	*Good morning, miss!*
Marnin, may anzum!	*Good morning, sir!*
Did yu zleep will?	*Did you pass a restful night?*
Ace. But yu dont arf znore.	*Yes, though you are a loud snorer.*

The Pub

My tong's that clisty yu could vile wood with er.	*I am thirsty.*
Right tiddly spot, seems like.	*Look! A public house!*
Where's the bar?	*Those look like bear droppings. Where is their owner?*
In the ceage.	*In his cage.*
Where's the bear?	*Where is the bar?*
Dru ere, meate.	*This way, friend.*
Paint a Devenish bee bee.	*Pint of bitter, please.*
Raight, skip.	*Certainly, sir.*
Wet yure ozzle with that ere.	*Get that down you!*
Ugh.	*What unusual beer.*
Blarst! 'Ere goes my glass.	*Alas! I have dropped my glass!*
Is 'er scat?	*Is it broken?*
Scat to scubmaw.	*Smashed to smithereens.*
Ar borgo mmimm monn hap garbo, didja ganny dinkler hor hor moy bewty?	*I am the village idiot.*
Oh ah.	*Really?*
There be wold Ernie.	*A friend has just entered the bar. Do excuse me, would you?*
Gart any vood?	*Is there any food?*
Gart a Plomun's.	*Ploughman's lunches are available.*
That lil skiddly bit er bird en cheese?	*That is a small Ploughman's lunch.*
Ol the tong.	*I do not like your attitude.*
Nur paint, ta.	*Another pint, please.*
Ee've ad enough.	*No.*
Gedzout, yu.	*Out.*
Wish'ee well.	*Good night.*

The Countryside

Purdy day.	*Fine day.*
Ace, breave and waarm.	*Yes, pleasantly mild.*
Ah. Zunny like.	*Yes, sunny too.*
Be them thur zhape?	*Are those sheep?*
No, them thur be turmuts.	*No, they are turnips.*
Be that thur tensive whaight?	*Is that a wheat prairie?*
No, that be Dirtmore.	*No, that is Dartmoor National Park.*
Wind's vrum westurd.	*It is raining.*
Wind's vrum easturd.	*It is cold.*
Wind's vrum norrurd.	*It is colder.*
Wind's vrum suthurrd.	*Nice day.*
Can we parrk 'ere?	*Is this a car park?*
Mebbe.	*Give me £1.*
Seafe beathing ere?	*Is it safe to bathe here?*
Be yu Ramblerrs?	*Are you members of the Ramblers Association?*
Ace, we be.	*Yes, actually.*
Ace, tis seafe beathing.	*No, it is not safe bathing.*
Er be vlat caam.	*There is no wind.*
Er be a bid of a breeze.	*There is a lot of wind.*
Er be a bid of a blow.	*It is blowing a gale.*
Er be a bit of popple.	*The sea is very rough.*
Er be plain robbly.	*Is that a tidal wave?*
Ace. Dirrdy wether.	*Ocean liners are running for shelter.*

Ladies and Gentlemen's Requisites

Marnin.	*Good day.*
Marnin, zur, madam, me startler.	*Good day sir, madam, sir.*
I nades vishun taykle.	*I would like some fishing tackle.*
This yur anny gude?	*Is this what you require?*
Baste inna wuld, vor sartin.	*It is an excellent make.*
Rop er up.	*Yes, that is suitable.*
Ow maich, me dear?	*How much is it?*
Whooart??	*That much?*
Two stun a arlies, plaze.	*28lb of new potatoes, please.*
Banch a sols, plaze.	*A bunch of daffodils, please.*
Ave yu crame be peast?	*Do you do clotted cream by post?*

He's a nice dross.	*What a charming frock.*
Yes she be.	*Yes, it is!*
I'll have im.	*I shall buy it!*
Ow mach be er?	*How much is it?*

Taboo Phrases

Arlies? Ay'll teak Jersay over Carnal anny dea.	*I prefer Jersey new potatoes to the Cornish model.*
Them Israelies be dooin prarperjarb with the darffs.	*I greatly admire the Israeli daffodil industry.*
Nabuddy du zpake Carnush namor.	*The Cornish language is mercifully extinct.*
Daivner Dumarra du live to Wailes.	*Daphne du Maurier lives in Wales.*
Ay bominates crame.	*I hate clotted cream.*
Marrgarine be god ver'ee.	*Margarine is good for you.*
Dem? Bain't that in Carnal?	*Isn't Devonshire part of Cornwall?*
Nowdies Zummerzet be part a Brisl, zee.	*Somerset is a suburb of Bristol nowadays.*
They melk quodies can du nathen bat gud.	*I am in favour of EEC milk quotas.*
Een Botham be a Yorkshireman.	*Ian Botham is a Yorkshireman.*
Tarnton be jest a wold relwa down.	*Taunton is just another railway town.*
Avalon? Er be a boozer, edna?	*Isn't Avalon a night club?*
Consarve Zedgemore.	*Sedgemoor must be conserved at all costs.*
Turble with the Zouth West is doo view garvanparks and doo much industry.	*The future of the South West lies with tourism alone.*

General

Vull a vurriners, nowdies.	*Our region is certainly popular with tourists.*
Zdiff with em, ale zummer.	*Most of them come between May and September.*

Air yu a coach turist?	*Are you a tourist?*
Noah, aim a urnery vurriner.	*No, I am a static holidaymaker.*
Ai be Carnish, ear yoe.	*I come from Cornwall.*
Ai be vrum Dem, edna?	*I come from Devon.*
Ai gum vrum Zummerzet, loike.	*I come from Somerset.*
Aim a Bristowlian, see.	*I come from Bristol.*
Which aerial?	*Whereabouts in Bristol?*
No ideal.	*I don't know.*
They be ail weird sapt us.	*There are great differences in the region.*
Laddow computers in Brisl.	*Bristol is prosperous.*
Laddow commuters in Zummerzet.	*Somerset is prosperous.*
Laddow caddle in Dem.	*Devon is prosperous.*
Laddow stanes in Carnal.	*Cornwall is not prosperous.*
They Corns du spraid lak hade lice.	*There are many young people in Cornwall.*
There's a laddow wark in Brisl.	*The South West is a growth area.*

Cider Talk

Whoart be zider a-mead av?	*What are the ingredients of cider?*
Vroot.	*Apples.*
Whoart typea vroot?	*What kind of apples?*
Foxwhelp, Kingston Blacks.	*Sour apples.*
Brownsnouts, Bloody Turks.	*Bittersweet apples.*
Zweet Alfords, Zweet Coppins.	*Sweet apples.*
Teaste one.	*Try one!*
Ecchh!	*Cider apples are rich in tannin.*
E be scrattin the vroot.	*He is mincing the apples.*

E be packin the cheezes.	*He is loading the pulp into bags.*
E be pressin the cheezes.	*He is crushing out the juice.*
E be teasten last year's.	*He is recruiting his strength.*
I allus wears may zider togs.	*Wearing a cricket jersey, corduroy trousers and army boots improves the must.*
Now I'm finin er with a daid ret.	*I am adding albumen to clear the brew.*
Er be workin.	*The juice is bubbling evilly.*
Er be ready.	*The juice has been bubbling evilly for three months.*
Put er in the zider wagon.	*Roll the barrel into the Austin A70 pickup.*
My grandad draenk zider, and e lived to be 110.	*Cider is often used in folk medicine.*
Wae burrid my brother at 31.	*It is dangerous to exceed the recommended dose.*

Caravan Site

Be there a garvan zite to Polbrathe?	*Is there a caravan site at Polbreath?*
Ace. Polbrathe bache, bay zoveneer zharp.	*Yes, on the beach by the newsagent.*
Zarry, vull. Trae Newky.	*Sorry, no vacancies. Try Newquay.*
Ae'd lak a stedak (tarrin) pech.	*I should like a static (touring) pitch.*
Ere be one andy for taylets.	*I have a nice one in the urinals.*
Ere be one with zay views.	*Here is one at the top of a steep hill.*
Ez ut zaafe?	*Why is the caravan balanced on that pinnacle of rock?*

Ace.	*It has not budged an inch since the gale blew it up there last Tuesday.*
May van be vull a waader.	*My caravan leaks.*
Then keep er out of the zee.	*It is not advisable to park on the beach while the tide is rising.*
This be a luvley site.	*This is a two acre field in an area of outstanding natural beauty, containing 20,000 pastel coloured caravans.*
Ye'm got a laddow luggage, nabor.	*Good morning, neighbour. Why is your caravan surrounded by three Cortinas and a ton of clothes pegs?*
Why yew carrying thet archin?	*What are you doing with that hedgehog?*
Tek zalt, pipper, claay . . .	*Take 1 pinch salt, pepper, 5lb clay . . .*
Wrop op yar archin . . .	*Season and swathe your hedgehog . . .*
Fire er in the stove . . .	*Throw it into the stove . . .*
Pull er out when e isses.	*Cook for 20 mins at Regulo 5.*
Smash im lak an aig and is guts vall vree.	*Crack it like an egg and its guts fall out.*
Mmmm!	*Fit for an Emperor!*
Wassamarrer? Yu a crank, meate?	*Are you a vegetarian?*
Them gippoes be garn.	*Our neighbours left in the night.*
Wheer be the cheelder?	*Have you seen the children?*

The Supernatural

Urk! What be that baayin'?	*Listen! What's that baying?*

Ow the geale do whistle on the Abbots Way.	*Only the wind in the dolmens.*
Tis a baad night to be abraad on Dirtmoor.	*This is no night for a girl to be walking on Dartmoor.*
Ace. On sich a night as this yur a man can yur the Yell Ounds.	*Yes. For that is the baying of the Hounds of Hell.*
Ear yoe, Watson! The gan!	*Quick, Watson! The revolver!*
And Aarthur. 'E do zlape and wait to come agin.	*King Arthur sleeps awaiting the Day.*
Baarn in Tintagel . . .	*Born in Tintagel . . .*
reased and reared in Camelot . . .	*lived in Cadbury Castle . . .*
med zpells with Marlin in Lyonnesse . . .	*trafficked with magicians on the seabed off Land's End.*
zailed with his wound to Avalon.	*sailed mortally wounded for Glastonbury.*
And e zhall come agin . . .	*He will return to save Somerset.*
and zeave Albion.	*We will need him after the retirement of Ian Botham.*

SOUTH

Introduction

THE CONVENTIONAL VIEW of the South of England is of Basingstoke, Portsmouth and Southampton, interspersed with tourist Meccas and stockbrokers. But not long ago, the countryside was littered with smock-frocked chawbacons. Thomas Hardy noticed several. And it is unreasonable to assume that just because they are no longer seen on the 8.40 to Victoria, they have become extinct. In the great emptinesses of Cranborne Chase and the New Forest, Salisbury Plain and those gravel pits you see from the M3 before you get to Basingstoke, ancient matters bear hard on the lives of modern men.

The visitor to the South of England must therefore remain on the *qui vive.* While it is safe to assume that the coastal strip will cause little trouble, there are sections inland where he will be severely taxed. A threatening silence may as easily descend on a public bar in Hampshire as on one among the great hills rolling up to West Dorset's Golden Cap. The traveller should prepare for his reserves of easy geniality to be plumbed to the bottom. The people of the Deep South are charming and hospitable but they prefer those who share their preoccupations — seedtime and harvest, perpendicular architecture, the care and management of the seaside boarding house. Nor for nothing did Stella Gibbons set her immortal *Cold Comfort Farm* in the South of England.

Pronunciation Note

The people of Hampshire (Hampshire Hogs) realise that to outsiders they tend to sound a bit mental. This is not because they are, but because they speak with large goldfishlike movements of the mouth and jaws. In Dorset, try to introduce a bee-like buzzing wherever possible. Elsewhere, note *progressive nasalisation* (see East Anglia — Introduction).

Travel

Mornen, goodnow.	*Greetings, my good man!*
Mornen, my zunny.	*Hello.*
Can 'ee tellus the rwoad for Dargester (Wingester, Zaalsbury)?	*Which way for Dorchester (Winchester, Salisbury)?*
Parn?	*What?*
Be'ee dunch?	*Are you deaf?*
Zorry, I be dunch.	*Sorry, can't hear, I'm deaf.*
But I d'know ow to read gobs.	*I can, however, lip read.*
Tes a goodish way.	*It is many days' journey from here.*
About of five miles.	*About twelve miles.*
You'd go aff the Downs (Chease).	*Off the Downs (Chase).*
Under th'birge athirt the rwoad . . .	*Under the bridge across the road . . .*

ower the knap . . .	*over the small hill . . .*
along bi the archets . . .	*through the orchards . . .*
(tes a shart cut-like) . . .	*(it's a short cut) . . .*
to where the halteran run zideland past the caamp . . .	*to where the path slants past the Roman camp . . .*
and ye be on the mean rwoad.	*and you're on the main road.*
God bless 'ee, zurs!	*Give me money for beer.*
Spladder the wold mummet.	*Choke the old image with wheel dust.*
Heh, heh, heh! Grockles!	*I do not like tourists.*
E never said nathen about no drongway.	*This narrow sheep path is not on our sketch map.*
What be thaat a-tissen?	*What's that hissing?*
Granada be a-bwilen.	*The car is boiling.*
Thet bludda twitten's plead wags with the conrods.	*That narrow track was suitable only for 4 wheel drive vehicles.*
Garbarettur's come abrode.	*The carburettor has come off.*
We'll vurlikely vreeze.	*We will probably freeze to death.*
Noah whope!	*That is unlikely in the circumstances.*
Parse the distinguisher.	*The fire extinguisher, please.*

Eating and Sleeping

Lookie thear! A tay sharp!	*Look! A teashop!*
Whear?	*Where?*
Overright the Tescoes.	*Opposite the supermarket!*
I be rather chippy.	*I am certainly hungry!*
We'll arve Darzet narbs . . .	*We will have crisp rolls . . .*
Trowbridge beacon, New Varest venzun . . .	*bacon, venison . . .*

bwiled neddles, Starkbridge trout . . .	*boiled nettles, trout . . .*
pill of melk, part of tay . . .	*a large jug of milk, pot of tea . . .*
and keep the pompey abwilin. Zet to!	*and keep the kettle boiling. Dig in!*
Moost mworish, them knotlins.	*Very addictive, those chitterlings.*
Give I a clumper o' ceake.	*Could I have a slice of cake?*
Fine and eger, than Blue Vinnie.	*Excellently sharp, that Blue Vinnie.*
Ay! You'm et up every bit and crimp!	*Oy! You've scoffed the lot!*
Ees. Virst bird the virst cass.	*The early bird catches the worm.*

Gart comadation?	*Have you a room for the night?*
Them sheets be vinnied.	*Those sheets are damp.*
We needs dewbit, brekfus, nuncheon, cruncheon, nammit, crammit, and zupper. And baid.	*We require full board.*

The Pub

I could tackle a pint.	*Shall we stop for a drink?*
Ees. I veels a turrible drowth.	*Yes, I am thirsty.*
How be 'ee?	*How are we, gentlemen?*
Pure, ta.	*Fine, thank you.*
Can I vetch'ee zummat?	*What would you like to drink?*
Pint er Pompey (Badger).	*Pint of bitter, please.*
Pint er sixex.	*Goodnight, Europe.*
Lookie that ere poor twoad.	*Look at that poor fellow.*
Lookie that there wold vuddicks.	*And that slatternly woman.*

Beath ad a nitch o'drink.	*They are both extremely drunk.*
Proper 'orridge in ere.	*Yes, this seems to be a place frequented by low characters.*
Pocket o' crips, ta.	*Packet of crisps, please.*
Vleavour?	*What kind of crisps?*
Zmokely bacon, jeeze en inon, praan cacktil, Barvil, zalten venegger.	*Smokey bacon, cheese and onion, prawn cocktail, Bovril, salt and vinegar.*
You arright?	*Are you quite well?*
Bit zweemish . . .	*Not quite the thing . . .*
My meat's took bad.	*My friend is ill.*
Off 'ee goes, then.	*Out, both of you.*

The Countryside

Twill be hart, teday.	*It will be a hot day.*
Howdie knaw?	*How do you know?*
Pride-of-the-marnin yander . . .	*There is a mist over there . . .*
Archets in blooth.	*The orchards are in flower.*
Grin buds on the hangens . . .	*Leaves are bursting in the woods on the hillside . . .*
Gullies empty, brooks vull.	*The ditches are empty but the streams are full.*
Boy Arry spreadin arn the cowleaze.	*Harry, 74, is muckspreading on the pasture.*
Twas my aunt's sisters' varm.	*This farm belonged to my ancestors.*
It baint carn cundry.	*It's not corn country.*
It baint caddle laand.	*It's not cattle country.*
But it's the pleace of my vore-vriends.	*But it's the place of my ancestors.*
Ees, un's hwome.	*Yes, it's home.*

And en gits zum gud ee yee see grants.	*And it is eligible for generous EEC grants.*
Planty tourists, too.	*Lots of tourists, too.*
And ale the venzun you can ate.	*And all the deer you can eat.*
Boat time I grubbed out some o' they drees, tho'.	*About time I chopped down some of those trees, though.*
Vary wold, Nee Varest.	*There is no place for the New Forest in modern agriculture.*

Ladies and Gentlemen's Requisites

Marnin, dacter!	*Good morning, doctor!*
How bee'ee?	*And how are we today?*
Only middlin, be gollikins!	*At death's door.*

I be shrowrod.	*A shrew ran over my foot, and left me lame.*
And when I do teak vood . . .	*When I eat . . .*
I do vetch up . . .	*I throw up . . .*
and I do urge and urge.	*and retch and retch.*
And I do have the brown typhus.	*I have bronchitis.*
Oh, ah. Teak two aspern.	*Dear me! Two aspirin.*

Bardle er aspern, ta.	*Bottle of aspirin, please.*
Ow my head do drub and quob.	*My head is throbbing.*
I leaft my toothbrush to hwome.	*I left my toothbrush at home.*
Toothy peaste ta.	*Toothpaste please.*
Ave 'ee spectacles? I be gone dark.	*Do you sell spectacles? I seem to have gone blind.*

Taboos

Ampshire Wiltshire and Darzit'll all be one coundy, somewhen.	*The South will someday become a single administrative unit.*
Ook's a vine spart vor commuterland.	*Hook is the ideal spot for a 5,000 home Private Enterprise Commuter Development.*
Basingstoke's a vine and purdy town.	*Basingstoke is the spiritual heart of England.*
I lives in the country, too. Zurrey, actual.	*I am also a countryman, from Surrey.*
Them there poilons looks very plazen.	*Those pylons give depth to what would otherwise be a rather boring view.*
Course, zee zailing be only for pastime.	*Ocean racing is a sport.*

Whart Bembridge warnts 'm a peer.	*Someone should build a pier, with amusements, at Bembridge.*
HMS Vactry? Boozer, baint en?	*Isn't HMS Victory a pub?*
Clever vellers, they Vree Wessexers.	*The Free Wessex Party is a little island of sanity in a mad, mad world.*
My granfer do mind Barnmith as a zand'll.	*200 years ago, Bournemouth was a sand dune.*
The Army've doo lettle land en Darzet (Wiltshire).	*The Army owns too little land in Dorset (Wiltshire).*

General

I be a zandel wearer.	*I am a keen naturalist.*
I likes zhells.	*I am a keen shell collector.*
Ave'ee tried Tyneham?	*The lost village of Tyneham is a favoured spot.*
Plaze zend an amblins.	*Please send an ambulance.*
My meate be sploded down Tyneham.	*My friend has been blown up while shell collecting.*
My meate be zhot a-orchiddin.	*My friend has been shot while collecting orchids on Salisbury Plain.*
My meate be gazzed aburdin.	*My friend has been nerve gassed while bird watching near Porton Down.*
My meate be vlattened a-vlintin.	*My friend has been run over by a cruise missile launcher while archaeologising near Tidworth.*
Nobaddy do go therr no morr.	*The Army is a powerful force for conservation.*

The Seaside Boarding House

Good morning.	*Hello, landlady!*
Yais?	*Hello, sir or madam!*
Got vacancies?	*Have you a room to let?*
Yais. Aitchansee, toot cunfert.	*Yes. Just like home, running water in all rooms.*
Do'ee comodate seniles?	*Do you accept permanent residents?*
Yais.	*Yes, many elderly folk come here to die.*
Passin away's extry.	*Dying is extra.*
I keep a naice respectible ouse.	*We have a commission deal with a firm of undertakers.*
Come along, ai avent got all day.	*If you would be so good as to follow, I will show you to your room.*
Oi! Wherezea zee view?	*Where is the sea view?*
Out the windy.	*Between the gasometer and the tannery.*
Ah. I zee 'un.	*I am focusing my powerful telescope . . . Ah!*
Ere! Wozzis?	*I have found a flea in my bed.*
Oney fleas in ere is wot you brot with you!	*Dear me! What an unprecedented disaster!*
Ere! Wozzat?	*There is a stranger sleeping in my bed!*
Werl, whaddyaspeck, forteen quid a nite?	*That is a double bed. Economics dictate that I fill the other half.*
Forrin, she be.	*Her name is Jutta, and she is a 19-year-old language student from Stockholm.*

Werl, justis once.	*I thought (wrongly) that those were her matched pair of hot water bottles. This is a most satisfactory arrangement.*
Werl, then.	*We aim to satisfy our guests.*
Tara for now.	*Sleep well.*

Thatched Cottage

This be a jarming caddage.	*What a charming cottage!*
Thankee, muss.	*Thank you, madam.*
Un's got cob walls.	*It has mud walls.*
Un be datched.	*It is thatched.*
Un's got meece, vurlikely.	*It has probably got mice.*
Th'wold cows be to th'ovel.	*Milk comes regularly.*
There be a plot o' garden-like.	*It has a small garden.*
Roses 'ave clumb up the parch.	*Roses festoon the porch.*
There be bloodywarriors . . .	*There are wall-flowers . . .*
Un's overrun, but there be still butter deasies . . .	*It's overgrown, but there are ox eye daisies . . .*
and oneyzuck, and pissabeds . . .	*Honeysuckle and dandelions . . .*
and crewels in the lawn.	*and cowslips in the lawn.*
You could give they brimmles a whang o' the swophook . . .	*You could give the brambles a slash . . .*
and pick that there cooch.	*and weed the potatoes.*
Mind you don't tear the swop-hook.	*Don't break the slasher.*
Mind you don't break your trousis.	*Careful you don't tear your trousers.*
Be that a musheroon in the privy?	*Is that a mushroom in the toilet?*
That bain't a musheroon, that be a tusheroon.	*No, a toadstool.*

I'll lend 'ee a pear a buts.	*I'll lend you some wellingtons.*
Un be grand round to dumps.	*It is charming at dusk.*
You can zit with the door ajor . . .	*You can sit with the door open . . .*
and look at the airmice when they do vlitter.	*and watch the bats.*
Doo undrid pound the zennit.	*£200 per week.*

Agriculture for Beginners (Pastoral)

I be a varmer.	*I am a farmer.*
Ged arf my land, will'ee.	*You are trespassing.*
This be my vambly.	*This is my family.*
This be my boy.	*This is my son and heir.*
Him drivin' the pickup.	*The one in the Subaru with the stickers.*
What be they?	*What do the stickers say?*
YOUNG FARMERS DO IT IN WELLIES	*YOUNG FARMERS DO IT INFREQUENTLY.*
WAKE UP WITH A YOUNG FARMER.	*DOZE OFF WITH A YOUNG FARMER.*
When be haymeaken?	*When will you make the hay?*
God bless'ee we doant meak heay namor.	*We no longer make hay, fool.*
We meakes zilage.	*We make silage.*
We nitrogens the grass til un be blue.	*We put nitrogen on the grass till it turns blue.*
Then we cuts un . . .	*We cut it . . .*
mixes un wi' sulphuric . . .	*mix it with sulphuric acid . . .*
chops un and clamps un.	*chop it up small and seal it in concrete bunkers.*
Caddle do love un.	*The cattle are not given anything else to eat.*
Cor! Whadda pong!	*It smells a bit, doesn't it?*

Har, har! Cundry smells.	*That's country life for you.*
Vine if you do wear a axygen marx.	*Fine as long as you wear protective clothing.*

Retirement Community

Nice day.	*The sun is almost shining.*
Yes, very nice.	*It is cold, grey and rainy.*
Bognor is always nice.	*We have come to the beach to die, you know.*
And handy for Arthur and Sharon.	*Our children come to see us sometimes.*
Yes, handy.	*Yes, sometimes.*
Quite handy, anyway.	*Well, every now and then.*
We had a lovely time with them Christmas.	*We used to go to them for Christmas, you know.*
It wasn't last Christmas.	*Yes. Not last Christmas.*
No, nor the one before.	*But recently.*
Of course they've other fish to fry.	*It's the children.*
Oh, you know, we're always so *busy*.	*Yes, it's the children.*
Bridge, W.I., Evergreens — we never stop.	*They don't have time for us old ones.*
Oh no, we don't dwell on the past.	*I mean George won the V.C. at Wipers.*
Eighty years young, that's us.	*And Enid used to be a music hall singer.*
We've got our life, they've got theirs.	*But why should they want to know?*
Both full up, chockablock.	*Why should we bother them with it?*
We've got the pitch and putt . . .	*They've got the telly . . .*
and the telly . . .	*and the garden . . .*
and the prom . . .	*and the car . . .*

and . . . er . . . well, you
know . . .

The Dunroamin Guest House
is very nice.

Handier than a house of our
own.

Specially when you get to
our age.

Capable woman that Mrs
Eagleton.

Very firm.

Well, she'll have tea on
the table.

See you again sometime.

and the house.

We lent them some money for
their house actually.

Poor things always seem too
busy to pay it back.

And when you get to our age
you don't mind sleeping
in . . .

separate dormitories.

Not much anyway.

Well, time we were going.

Nice to talk to someone young.

SOUTH EAST

Introduction

THE ROMAN INVASION and the Norman Conquest are only two of the many influences that Southeastern English has had to soak up. These dramatic events have made the region the cradle of Standard English, true; but they have also put the language of the South East several months ahead of the rest of Great Britain. This must have been baffling in 1070 A.D.: it is even more so in the 1980s, where the invasions are continuous, resupply being through Heathrow and Gatwick. Things change too fast to be kept up with.

There is, however, a true Southeastern culture, many-layered and diverse, underlying the frenzied surface activity. It is complicated: the high incidence of insanity and drunkenness among the thatched cottages of Surrey and the gladiolus-spiked vistas of Croydon is a measure of the fact that even the natives don't get it right all the time.

It is only in the parts of the region not yet hit by commuterdom that pre-Norman dialects survive. While there certainly are parts of Kent, Sussex and the Home Counties inhabited by aborigines, they are very hard to find. The main pockets of dialect are in London, particularly in the sections judged by estate agents to be beyond redemption or anyway too far from public transport and hospital casualty departments.

The inhabitants of South East England are particularly sensitive to appearances. In other regions, splashes of mud, agricultural and marine odours can be of value in breaking the ice. The non-aboriginal South East sets much store by *respectability* (Marks & Spencer) and the aboriginal sectors in *sharpness* (Burton's).

Pronunciation Note
General South Eastern language is pronounced without much movement of the lips and with an air of complacency. Aboriginal dialects in the London area gain conviction from an assumed speech defect, e.g. a lisp, "w" for "r", "f" for "th".

Travel

Ow do I git to Lundin?	*I wish to go to London.*
Stition.	*The station is round the corner.*
Ahem.	*That is my seat.*
Uh-uh.	*No, I reserved it. Look, here is the ticket.*
Ahem.	*Listen, you smug bastard, I sit in that seat every morning.*
Ahem.	You, *as I say, are sitting in* my *seat.*
Hraashm.	*If I had a gun I would shoot you.*
Rustle.	*As it is, I am shaking my FT at you.*

Tch!	*Will you stop shoving, scum!*
Wheredjathinkyoregoin?	*No entry to the underground without a ticket.*
London Transport are pleased to announce the imminent arrival of train for Victoria, Temple, etc.	*The Circle Line train is stuck in a tunnel.*
Sniff.	*I have a severe cold.*
Sniff.	*If you sit next to me you will become infected.*
Hi! My name is Tony and this is Cheryl.	*We are bronzed colonials.*
Mind if I rest my backpack on your lap?	*We are unspeakable.*
Is this the stop for the Tower of London?	*We have arrived at Gloucester Road.*
Yes.	*No.*

Eating and Sleeping

Oh look! A Stike Ouse.	*There is a restaurant!*
Give us a stike, ta.	*I would like a three-course meal.*
Give us a big stike, ta.	*I have just got out of prison (the Foreign Legion, Saudi Arabia).*
Yes, sir.	*I shall return bearing prawn cocktail, rump steak, chips, peas and tomatoes, and a portion of false fruit salad with ice cream.*
Very nice.	*Acceptably bland.*
Ere! Wozzis? Biroes?	*Someone left a bunch of asparagus on my plate.*
Forrin muck.	*I know what I like.*

Oh look! A restrong.	*I have sighted e.g. the Bistro Charles de Gaulle, Esher.*

O God forrin muck.	*Could we not go to the steak house?*
You reely liked that place in Benidorm.	*No.*
Yais, flowers?	*Hello, sir and madam.*
Super lwognin.	*Washing up water with a hint of flannel.*
Cock o' vin.	*Broiler au Bisto.*
Paish Melber.	*False fruit with ice cream.*

Let's go down the Musso.	*Shall we dine at the Trattoria Benito Mussolini, Penge?*
Ecco prosciutto esperanto mama mia, bugatti formosa!	*Evenin' all, Mick from Sydenham your maitre d' in full control!*
Ooh!	*He ran his hand up my leg! Cheeky thing!*
All right, luv.	*Quiet, Tony.*
Antipasto.	*Tinned sardines, Hellman's, slice of garlic sausage.*
Spaghetti.	*Spaghetti al Dentine.*
Copa Bocaccio.	*False fruit with ice cream.*

The Pub

Evenin, all!	*Good morning (evening, night).*
What's yours, Tony?	*Might I buy you a drink?*
The usual, Jack.	*Indeed. You know what it is.*
Two pints of wallop, landlord.	*Two pints of weak Courage beer, please.*
What's your poison, Jimmy?	*What would you like to drink?*
My shout, squire!	*It is my turn to order.*
Lay something on the ale, eh?	*Perhaps some food?*
Ploughman's, ta John.	*Bread and cheese, please.*
Frenchman's, ta John.	*Bread and artificial pâté, please.*

Peasant's, ta John.	*Bread, please.*
Pervert's, ta John.	*Where is the gents?*
Ha hwa hwa hwa.	*I am feigning amusement.*
Did you hear the one about the nun and the bulldozer?	*I am about to tell a revolting joke.*
Yes.	*I do not wish to hear it.*
I am in training.	*I am off alcohol for sporting reasons.*
I am in training for Christmas.	*I am drinking constantly.*
Where's the knights, plugs, dwarves?	*Where is the gents?*
Where's the damsels, sockets, snowwhites?	*Where is the ladies?*
Where is the exit?	*I have just become a teetotaller.*
Night, all!	*I cannot stand any more of this.*

The Countryside

The South East is geologically fascinating.	*There are a lot of motorways round here.*
There are many significant features.	*Some motorways pass through very nice areas.*
Please show me the significant features.	*Which ones?*
There is the Thames Valley.	*There is the M4.*
The Thames Valley is a fertile plain.	*Near the M4 are power stations and Slough.*
There are the North Downs.	*There is the M27.*
There is the Coastal Strip.	*There is a huge retirement community.*
The Weald of Kent is geologically uninteresting.	*Nobody has yet managed to build a motorway across the Weald.*
There is the Thames Estuary.	*There is the biggest cesspool in Europe.*

The geology of the region is constantly evolving.	*We are building a motorway box round London.*
Dinosaurs are found in the region.	*There are pockets of ignorance.*
But progress cannot be gainsaid.	*The Government is selling the Green Belt to developers.*
Population patterns are changing.	*Inner London is now inhabited by Communist muggers and I do not wish to live there.*

Ladies and Gentlemen's Requisites

John sent me.	*I am a person of standing.*
Big John sent me.	*I am a person of considerable standing.*
Could I 'ave some fags?	*10,000 Players, please.*
Lookin very well, today.	*I see that both your legs are broken.*
Cor someone 'as didded a pony.	*This shop smells of fear.*
Seen Maurice lately?	*Have you been six feet below the surface of Fulham cemetery lately?*
Nice bloke, Maurice. Pity about the er, genitals.	*Maurice tried to fob us off with Silk Cut.*
Well, can't stay chatting all day. Tara, then.	*I must pop down the road for some cigarettes.*

Psst!	*Excuse me?*
Waana score some smack, coke, speed, grass?	*Would you like to buy some baking powder, cornflour, aspro, oregano?*
Right man. How much?	*Yes, willingly! How much?*
What is this bullshit, man?	*This is the first time I have sniffed fizzy heroin, cocaine, speed.*
Gimme back the bread.	*Could I possibly have a refund?*

Hrrrargh.	*Good morning, hairdresser.*
Ow wud we lake our air cut, sir?	*How would you like your hair cut?*
Snaargh.	*In absolute silence.*

Hello, sweetie.	*I can't remember your name.*
Gavin'll be with you in ten seconds.	*You are not important enough to get a haircut from me.*
Living in the country are you?	*You look as if you have recently popped out of a hayrick.*
*Fab*ulous!	*Oh.*
Your usual?	*Would you like a trim?*
Have you tried seaweed/river mud/bleach/antelope's placenta?	*We have ways of making trims more expensive.*
Mmm, super.	*Oh.*
Er, Gavin . . .	*Good God! What have you done!*
Don't you like it, sweetie?	*Strewth! Did I do that?*
We've all got it like that.	*Baldness is* très chic, *this year.*
See you next year, then.	*It'll look lovely when it's grown out.*
Something for the weekend?	*Can I sell you some contraceptives?*

A Day Out in the Green Belt

Well, Snatcher, it's orf to the country.	*We are having a day out of London.*
Bromley's nice.	*We are in the suburbs.*
Nice semis.	*What large, charming houses!*
I'm frightened.	*I feel the beginnings of agoraphobia.*
Relax, Snatch. We're in Wentworth.	*We are now in desirable Surrey.*
'Op up in this tree.	*From this hide, we can watch stockbrokers.*
There in them pink flowers . . .	*Those stockbrokers are in their rose garden.*
Sweaty, inney?	*They have just played tennis.*
They'll start the owsyefarver soon.	*Soon they swap wives.*
Andy, the Norf Downs.	*The rolling hills of Surrey are ideal for our purposes.*
Ere's ve bird . . .	*Here is a stockbroker's moll.*
Orright, darlin, youn meese goin for a liddle ride . . .	*Please step this way.*
EEK!	*Oh! A man in a mask.*
Inna motor.	*Please get into the car.*
Goo' mornin Mister Rothschild, we ave got your missis.	*Sir, we are holding your wife.*
Listen, John, I'm in Deptford.	*My window overlooks the gasworks, the Thames.*
Er, nice work, Enid.	*How clever of you to find a telephone.*
Heeelp!	*Please send assistance.*
It's a fair cop, guvner.	*We will come quietly.*
Say tara to the sun, Chummy.	*You will get five years for this, Snatcher.*

Who's Who

Thank goodness we have moved to Bromley.	*By doubling the mortgage we have fled Pinner.*
Yes, we love the old Cortina.	*The post of Mailroom Superintendant does not provide a company car.*
Of course Reg will get a company car next year.	*Reg is being kicked sideways.*
They know they can't do without him.	*Unless of course he is made redundant.*
We like to think we keep our end up.	*Reg washes the car every Sunday morning.*

We love living in the country.	*We live in the suburbs of Dorking.*
One meets such interesting people.	*Our next door neighbour is a bank manager.*
Variety's the spice of life, I always say.	*On the other side we have an actuary.*
Don't you, dear?	*If you do not agree I will give you hell later.*
Yes, dear.	*I wonder if I could sneak off to the pub?*

I drive a Granada Estate.	*I am a rep.*
I drive a Citroen.	*I am a teacher or Friend of the Earth.*
I drive a Jag.	*I am keen on engineering, particularly my secretary's.*
I get around in the Roller.	*I am of interest to the police.*
I drive an old MGB.	*I am of interest to nobody except my girlfriend Miranda.*

Have a beer, John boy (Doris girl).	*We have a limitless cocktail bar in the lounge room.*

Dolores is on the tennis court.	*We have a tennis court.*
Scott is in the Jacuzzi.	*We have a whirlpool bath.*
It's a long way up from Canning Town.	*Once, life was not so beautiful.*
But do we change?	*But my personality shines undimmed.*
I've got a hundred suits in the wardrobe.	*I have wealth beyond the dreams of avarice.*
But have I changed?	*But my simple soul glows radiantly as ever.*
No, you have not changed.	*You are as always entitled to your own opinion.*

London Conversation

Ello John. What d'you reckon?	*Good morning, Aloysius. Is it not a delightful day?*
Ello John. What d'you reckon?	*Indeed, Tarquin. The birds are singing, the sun shining. Crystal Palace's Cup prospects have never looked brighter.*
I dunno. What d'you reckon?	*You are perfectly correct. All, as Pangloss once said, is for the best in the best of all possible worlds.*
I dunno. What d'you reckon?	*I personally tend to the opposite view, also set out by Voltaire in his anti-Leibnizian work* Candide.
I dunno. What d'you reckon?	*Yes, this view has its merits. But naturally each of us is entitled to draw his own conclusions. After all, we live in a dangerous world . . .*

I dunno. What d'you reckon?	*As Voltaire points out through his mention of the Lisbon earthquake of 1755.*
I dunno. What d'you reckon?	*Precisely! And we are forced to conclude with Voltaire's hero that all that remains is for each of us to occupy himself with his immediate concerns: to, as it were,* cultivate his garden.
Yeah. Tara, then.	*Quite! Well, Tarquin, you have certainly given me much to mull over. Thank you!*
Tara, then.	*Not at all! It is through discussion and controversy that Literature pours forth its treasures! Now, farewell!*

London Street Cries

Ere! Missis! Mister!	*Excuse me!*
Piss off, John.	*I do not require any such goods.*
Arf a dollar.	*This costs twelve and a half pence.*
Oo will start me at arf a dollar?	*Will anyone offer me twelve and a half pence?*
Channel noomero sank.	*Decanted after-shave lotion.*
Fowdy numberella.	*Iranian war surplus parachutes.*
Speshil import.	*Fell off the back of a lorry.*
Digitilwotch.	*Digital watch.*
Arf a bar, ven.	*50p then.*
Awright make it a note.	*All right, £1.*
One single sheet for vis.	*£1 only for this aftershave, parachute, digital watch.*

I am robbin myself.	*I am making a huge profit.*
Fiver, ven. Tenner.	*Give me five pounds, ten pounds.*
Gemmun over ere sez a pony.	*My accomplice there says £25.*
Fank you, sir, and you, madim. And you, effendi.	*Thank you, punters of all nations.*
Find ve lady, chief?	*Let us try an innocent game with these three cards.*
Easy, innit? Ere's your money.	*You have just won five pounds.*
Deerodeer odeer. Arnlarky.	*You have just lost £40.*
Try agen?	*Let us go on.*
Piss off, I doan want your rahnveahses.	*As a concession to decency I will allow you to keep your trousers.*

EAST

Introduction

EASTERN ENGLAND IS a land cloaked in mystery, susceptible to sea fogs, biting east winds, and sudden outbursts of opera. Its rolling pastures, US Air Force bases and wheat prairies are inhabited by a ruggedly independent race, insensitive to extremes of temperature.

It will not escape the linguist's attention that parts of East Anglia are as close to Denmark as they are to London, and that the North Sea can be a good deal easier to travel than the A10 and 11, particularly between six and ten on Fridays and Sundays. During the Dark Ages the inhabitants of Denmark were quick to take advantage of this, rushing to and fro and leaving large chunks of their speech behind them. Even now, experts aver that the inhabitants of Norfolk are more readily understood by the Friesian Islanders than by speakers of Standard English.

Pronunciation Note
East Anglian pronunciation is not difficult for Standard English speakers, providing they follow the spellings given and observe two simple rules.

1. *The Rising Inflection*
The last word of the sentence is normally spoken a fifth above its predecessors, unless it is "bor", in which case the penultimate word and the "bor" both belong on the fifth. This makes all East Anglian utterances sound disconcertingly interrogative, until you get the hang of it.

2. *Progressive Nasalisation*
In the deep East Anglian countryside, there is a broad openness to the speech. The closer you get to a centre of population, the more nasal the speech becomes. Duplicate this by sticking your fingers up your nostrils. Use your initiative: for example, one finger is probably adequate in a town like Blofeld (Bluefailed), between Norwich and Yarmouth; while in Ipswich, two digits should be rammed in to the knuckles. If you feel shy, hold a handkerchief over your face while speaking.

Travel

Hilloo, bor!	*Excuse me!*
Oi oont noo where I em.	*I am lost.*
Blass that int noo bledda good.	*Oh dear.*
Em oi a gooin to Haysbra?	*Is this the way to Happisburgh?*
Noo, yew've now come from Snitcham.	*No, you have just been through Snettisham.*
Bogger oi though that wer Windam.	*Dear me! I thought it was Wymondham.*
That fare to be daak.	*It is getting dark.*

Thass loonly hare in the Brecks.	*The Norfolk-Suffolk borders are a sparsely populated region.*
There int noo hootil afor Brendin.	*There are few tourist facilities.*
Yew kin com down ours if yew want.	*I offer you the hospitality of my humble abode.*
Kin oi put moy exe (gon, claver) in the back seat?	*Can I put my luggage in the back seat?*
Oi allus did loike blondes (brunettes).	*You are very pretty.*
Dew yew tun lift.	*Turn left.*
Dew yew tun roight.	*Turn right.*
Oo dare, thass brook.	*Oh, dear, the car has broken down.*
Blodda fen bilt's wore up.	*The fan belt is worn out.*
Tike arf yar toits.	*Remove your tights.*
Dew yew hare that owd wol a tootin?	*It is lonely and mysterious here.*
That du call to moind the wind in the tower at Hellesdon.	*It reminds me of my time in the mental hospital.*
Dew yew moind, bor!	*Stop it!*
Dew yew loy dun.	*Lie down.*
Com bek!	*Come back!*
Helloo moy dares!	*Evenin', all!*
Dare be praze, a carper!	*Thank goodness, a policeman!*
Hev yew sin a lewny a-ronnin?	*We are searching for an escaped lunatic.*
Shey wint thet awye.	*She went that-a-way.*

Eating and Sleeping

Blast I am ravished.	*I am extremely hungry.*
Hair yew are, a caff.	*Look! A restaurant.*
How do, mess.	*Good day, waitress.*

A foo wilkes.	*A few whelks.*
A Croomer crayb.	*A Cromer crab.*
Copla darzen wuysters.	*Two dozen oysters.*
That int a eyter crayb.	*That is not the edible crab* Cancer pagurus.
Thass a gilly.	*That is the Shore Crab* Carcinus maenas.
Oon't you ate that hair.	*Don't eat that.*
You'll git quare.	*You will be ill.*
I think I'll hev a cup a tey.	*I think I'll have a cup of tea.*
Bowel a shackles.	*A bowl of soup.*
Sleb a brid . . .	*A slice of bread . . .*
Slare on the butter . . .	*Lash on the butter . . .*
Dust a sugar.	*A sprinkling of sugar.*
Blast that snew grob.	*That was a large meal.*
Are ye fit?	*Ready?*
Hair we goo.	*We're off!*

Dew yew dew bay en bay?	*Have you a bed for the night?*
Dew yew mind sheerin with the tarkies?	*Do you mind sharing with the turkeys?*
Blast thass brass monkies.	*It is very cold.*
Thass blooin from the aste.	*The east wind is blowing.*
Bot we gart sintral hatin.	*But we have recently planted another row of oaks in the windbreak.*

The Pub

Droy wark, hooin bate.	*Hoeing beet makes you thirsty.*
How are you a-gooin arn?	*Evening, landlord.*
Bitter en yew, boy the look arn it.	*Good evening.*
Point a Bullids, ta.	*Unhappily, we are in Norfolk.*

Point a Adnams.	*Thank goodness we are in Suffolk, Essex.*
Chairs.	*Your very good health.*
Hair's hew, bor.	*And yours.*
Blodda hill, that ent a point.	*You have poured me short measure.*
Yare a gooin to git wrong.	*You are heading for trouble.*
Hey's paalatic.	*He is very drunk.*
Jasus Mary and Joseph, give us a lairge Jamesons and a slimloine limnead.	*I have popped over from Newmarket.*
Will, I'm arf to wark.	*I must go to work.*
But thass cloosin toime.	*But it is 11 p.m.*
Soo that is. Moind how ye goo, bor.	*So it is. 'Bye now.*
Moind how ye goo.	*Goodbye.*
Hay's a-gooin after the raabuts.	*He is off to catch rabbits.*
Larng-tailed raabuts.	*Pheasants.*

The Countryside

In the winter I wuk as a brusher.	*In the winter I work as a beater.*
I mind one night that snew a rum'un.	*One night it snowed hard.*
Yis, that snew pourin.	*Snow had fallen, snow on snow.*
Before that milted, Boy Aathur croop in the wod	*Before it melted, my friend Arthur crept into the wood.*
Hay's a rare owd boy for pheasants.	*He is a pheasant expert.*
Ah, an artful owd cup o' tea.	*Yes, a cunning man.*
That was frazin fit to flea a flint.	*It was freezing hard.*
He druv hes coe to the soide of the wod.	*He drove his cow to the side of the wood.*

He drug in a big owd sek.	*He dragged in a large sack.*
Thim bards was gooin arf like one o'clock.	*Pheasants were shooting about everywhere.*
That was terrified a pheasants.	*The place was thick with them.*
Thin hay did see the kayper a-comin.	*Then he saw the gamekeeper approaching.*
So he did toy thet sek onder the coe.	*So he tied the sack under the cow.*
How that did bleare!	*How it mooed!*
Up com the kayper, smart as a carrot.	*The keeper, an officious man, approached him.*
"That fare to snoo agin," say Aaathur.	*"Looks like more snow," said Arthur.*
"That fare to rine carpers," say the kayper.	*"It will soon be raining policemen," said the keeper.*
"I doubt you'll git a wristed."	*"I expect you will get arrested."*
Soo Aathur, hay laaf.	*Arthur laughed.*
"Missus'll hev dinner ready agin I git to ours," hay say.	*"My wife will have dinner ready by the time I get home," he said.*
Thin arf hay goo.	*And off he went, with the cow.*
Thay lie too thick, yew couldn't say noo bag.	*The snow was so thick you couldn't see the bag.*
Ah.	*Oh.*
I like a pheasant. That eat excellent.	*I think pheasant tastes delicious.*

Ladies and Gentlemen's Requisites

Marnin, darkter.	*Good morning, doctor.*
Moy hend (lig, too, hid) is quare.	*I have damaged my hand (leg, toe, head).*
Do thet hut, bor?	*Any pain?*
Thet do give me bossacks.	*Yes.*
Thet bulk loike blizes.	*It throbs severely.*
What heppen, bor?	*How did it happen?*
Th'owd dicka stood arnut.	*The donkey stood on it.*
Oi dagged en wid me fork.	*I stuck my fork into it.*
Oi'll give yer titnis jeb . . .	*This is a tetanus injection . . .*
and ye'll be adewin in a day'r soo.	*and you will be as right as rain.*
Hew's missis agooin on?	*I trust your wife is well?*
Ah, shay's agooin to be ill.	*Yes, she's expecting a baby.*
She dew kip raisin this hair owd glut.	*She is troubled with phlegm.*
Dew yew fitch me in a spissy man.	*Please bring me a specimen.*
Blast that hom a bit.	*Goodness! She seems to have an infection.*
Oo dare that one were far the vit.	*Dear me, wrong bottle.*
Dew yew tike a lok anniehoe.	*Send it off anyway.*

Taboos

Earal spryin? Thass maavulous for kids.	*A little bit of aerial crop spray is good for growing children.*
Consarve the Braads.	*Preserve the Broads.*
Plew op the Braads.	*Plough up the Broads.*
Thass toe much weight in Yewrup.	*There is too much wheat in Europe.*

Thass tew many owd charches rewnd hair.	*Bulldoze redundant churches.*
Thass tew foo earports rewnd hair.	*Viva Stansted!*
Es that a if one elivin?	*Is that an atom bomber?*
Yis, thass the sound of Fraydim.	*Yes. Wonderful sound, is it not?*
Brendin en Fikenum shud be a Noocler Fray Zoon.	*Brandon and Fakenham should be Nuclear Free Zones.*
Thass hoily flet.	*What flat countryside!*
Thass cooled.	*What a chilly climate!*

General

Blast thass flet!	*What flat countryside!*
Noo that ent.	*It is not flat.*
Es that a rarever?	*Is that a river?*
Noo, thass a drine.	*No, it is a drain.*
Hair com the hells.	*We are approaching the heights of Central Norfolk.*
That look flet to me.	*Looks pretty flat from here.*
Thass a aptic lucian.	*Optical illusion.*
Hair com the Bricks.	*We are entering the pine-clad Brecklands.*
Blass thass flet.	*They seem very flat.*
That ent flet, that rool.	*No, they are rolling.*
Looka thim hair rice harses.	*Look! Racehorses!*
Flet?	*Flat?*
Noo, staplechisers.	*No, steeplechasers.*
Whazza rarekit?	*Why is that brewery singing?*
Awbra Fistible.	*It's the Aldeburgh Festival.*
Hey oont sound verra will.	*That man singing sounds ill.*
Ah, but hey ent flet.	*Yes, but he is not flat.*
Bootifle city, Cambridge.	*A fine city, Cambridge.*

Nart toe helly.	*Nice and flat.*
Whale starp for a bare.	*Let's stop for a beer!*
Thass flet.	*The beer has lost its sparkle.*
Thass mint tobey flet.	*It is meant to be like that.*

The Essex Marshes

Thass rinin.	*It is raining.*
Thass blooin.	*There is much wind.*
Thass cooled.	*The wind has come full toss from the Urals.*
The mod'll drewn ye.	*The mud is very deep.*
Dew yew sty arn the cahzy.	*Stay on the causeway.*
Thass sampher.	*That is samphire.*
Thass say levender.	*That is sea lavender.*
Thass plaastic bartles.	*Those are plastic bottles.*
Thass a newcular power stition.	*That is a nuclear power station.*
Noo swemmun.	*It is dangerous to bathe.*
The bache es oopen Tharsdas.	*The beach is closed every day except Thursdays.*
Whoy's that cloosed?	*Why?*
Thass the Army (Nivy, Ear Force).	*It is used to test poison gas (missiles, new pilots).*
Whass thet bard?	*What is that bird?*
Thass a Brint Ghose.	*A Brent Goose.*
Whoy's that chookin?	*Why is it coughing?*
That grize nare the ringe.	*10,000 Brent Geese graze on the poison gas range.*
Thass oonly a marsh.	*Marshes have little commercial value.*
Thass poisoned with bards.	*Birds teem on the marsh.*

Agriculture, Arable

Whoy's your coat rarted arf arn you, bor?	*Why is the coat rotted off your back?*
I bin wartchin the sprie pline.	*I have been supervising aerial spraying.*
Whass he sprying?	*What is being sprayed?*
Round up and pair a quat, DDT, Igent Arange.	*Glyphosate and paraquat, DDT, 2,4,5-T.*
Where's he a-sprying?	*What is being sprayed?*
Effin Iss iss iss eye.	*Site of Special Scientific Interest.*
Es that laygle?	*Is that legal?*
Yes, thass laygle pinding dinegeld.	*Yes, if you do it while the committee is deciding how much to bribe you.*
Dare oo dare thass hard, farming.	*The plight of British agriculture is a sorry one.*
Ah. Hev a little cavyer?	*Yes. A little caviar?*
Noo, just parped in whoile they parlished the Rooler.	*No, I only popped in while they were polishing the Rolls.*
How's the boy?	*How is your heir?*
Hay's a carmunist.	*The other day he spoke admiringly of Central Government.*
Hay's a hoomersexal.	*The other day he spoke admiringly of a hedgerow.*
Hay's a dye boy now.	*He commutes from Cambridge to Eton by helicopter.*
Hay's a dooin well.	*Having become tired of his hamster he poisoned it with Warfarin.*
Dew yew hev a poile of land?	*Do you have much land?*
500 acres.	*One field.*
2000 acres.	*Four fields.*

5000 acres.	*One large field.*
Hey's a small farmer.	*He is a very rich dwarf.*

USAF Base

Howdy.	*Hello.*
USAF Lakenheath, have a nice day.	*Hello.*
We have a woodshed — F1/11 interface situation.	*One of your jet planes has crashed into my woodshed.*
This situation is in a usualisation mode.	*Oh my God not again!*
Evidently I am distressised.	*I am sorry about this.*
Unhappily this carries no apology capability mewise.	*But there is nothing I can do.*
I am putting you on hold.	*I am looking up your dossier.*
I am putting you on Muzak.	*I am giving the Special Branch your telephone number.*
Transferring you.	*Now you will speak to a CIA representative.*
Re my woodshed — F1/11 interface situation . . .	*As I was saying . . .*
Madam, your woodshed died for freedom.	*Madam, I am trying to put you in the wrong.*
In war woodsheds are expendable.	*I regard you as a piffling aboriginal.*
We must not place chickens before liberty.	*A murrain on your livestock.*
There is an air-breathing intermediate nuclear deterrent in my zucchini.	*There is a cruise missile in my courgettes.*
We are fighting a war here.	*I do not care.*
Our forces are fully committed.	*1% of our men are flying planes and the rest are getting drunk or whining about the weather.*

Please stage a recipient-motivated return to base.	*Please bring the cruise missile back.*
Madam, what you suggest is not only impossible but anti-patriotic.	*The cruise missile will not fit.*
Excuse me.	*This conversation has become tedious.*
Excuse me, I have to go push a button.	*Goodbye, world.*
Have a nice four minutes, now.	*Goodbye.*

Interview with a Dumpling

Thow'd gel hev made a foo dumplins.	*My wife has made us ten dumplings.*
Thow'd gel hev made several dumplins.	*My wife has made us one hundred dumplings.*
Cor teh heck.	*O gosh.*
Blass thass a master great dumplin.	*What a huge dumpling.*
I feel a bit peckewlier.	*I am feeling rather ill.*
You're a gooin to get wrong.	*My wife will be offended.*
Hair she com.	*I hear her approaching.*
Whass wrong wi thet gret haystack?	*What is wrong with our guest?*
He's now gone and went.	*He has just left suddenly.*
Blass thass a rum'un.	*How odd.*
Blass that *is* a rum'un.	*Yes,* indeed.
Must hev bin took quare.	*Look, he left a dumpling on his plate.*
Drog op noohow!	*What bad manners!*

WALES

Introduction

STANDARD ENGLISH speakers are often uncomfortably aware that their forebears have done their share of downtreading among the hills and valleys of Wales. There is a tendency to want to make it all better by being extra nice to these dark and stunted little folk.

But it is hard to be extra nice to a collection of people who fall ominously silent every time you enter a pub or a grocery shop. It is even harder to be extra nice when they resume their conservation not in the relatively pure English they were using before your intrusion, but in Welsh. It is easy, faced with this, to end up hurt and embittered. The Welsh, who after all have lost every battle since the beheading of Llewellyn ap Gruffydd, have an aggravating habit of behaving as if they had *won*.

And in a way, they have. Ever since the first Tudor slunk out of Wales to become King of England, the Welsh have consistently come out on top via the fire escape of history. Look at Lloyd George, or any of the other silver-tongued parliamentarians, poets and geniuses who have sneaked across the border. Standard English Speakers may let the Severn Bridge rot away, install 100% unemployment by decree, and nip off on holiday to Frinton. But when they return to their seat of office, rubbing their hands, they will find a Welshman seated in their chair, humming the Treorchy Male Voice Choir's Greatest Hits. There is no winning against the Welsh, so give up trying.

Pronunciation Note
The English spoken in Wales is a notoriously sing-song affair. The speaker should pretend to be suppressing an acute attack of hiccups. Men should speak with slitted eyes and lips thrust forward, while women should assume a smile of tremendous sweetness.

The Welsh language proper is difficult to pronounce as well as to learn. A rough approximation is, however, supplied in Emergency Welsh (page 64).

Travel

Wherr awy?	*Where are we?*
Doont knoo.	*I don't know.*
Ills everywhere.	*Mountains everywhere.*
Iss that a droad?	*Is that a road?*
Moose ton likely.	*Most unlikely.*
A trrack, more.	*More like a track.*
Look there, a druss tick!	*Look, a person!*
Esscuce me!	*Excuse me!*
Esscuce me, look!	*Er, excuse ME!*
YOU!	*OI!*
Was you callin me, was it?	*So sorry, I did not realise you were addressing me.*
What you want, then?	*Can I help?*

Owdo I get to Betsy Coed?	*Please direct me to Bettws-y-Coed.*
Teck the firs left, look.	*First left . . .*
Dright at Jones Fish . . .	*right at the fishmonger . . .*
oover thyill . . .	*over the hill . . .*
past the pit, there . . .	*past the coal mine . . .*
and you'll see a board says goomri . . .	*and you'll see a sign saying CYMRU . . .*
if you lookatit from the back, like.	*if you look at it from behind.*
Well go past the sign . . .	*Go past the sign . . .*
and sod off back to England where you belong.	*then you will be on your way home.*

Eating and Sleeping

Look! A caffy, Taffy!	*I have sighted a restaurant.*
There's grreat, now!	*Oh, goodie!*
I'm bladdi starved.	*I am very hungry.*
Ello mam!	*Good afternoon, waitress.*
I'll ave leek porridge.	*Please bring me boiled and macerated leeks.*
Nice leg o' lamb . . .	*Radnorshire lamb.*
What would you ave, mam?	*What are the specialities of the house?*
A clean tongue and a good conscience.	*That is my business.*
Which out o' the two, though?	*Please make a recommendation.*
I bin in fastin and penitence since my Ifor was took beyond.	*If you insist, though I never eat here myself.*
Bocket o' limpets.	*Some shellfish.*
Laver bread.	*Boiled and fried seaweed.*
Salmon.	*Tinned salmon.*

Porched salmon.	*Salmon poisoned with cymag.*
Boiled salmon.	*Poached salmon.*
Bara tato, with butter.	*Buttered potato bread.*
Bara brith.	*Spotty bun.*
And a nice drrink of buttermilk.	*I am off to the pub after, Sunday or no.*
I am lookin for a bard for the night.	*I am an eisteddfoddie.*
Aveyou gotta droom?	*Can I sleep here?*
Biyanbi kweck quid.	*B&B six pound.*
We ave cawl for breakfast.	*For breakfast we serve a traditional broth of fat bacon and vegetables, decorated with marigold blooms.*
Wgh.	*I shall be leaving earlier than that.*

The Pub

Evenin' all.	*Please resume your conversation.*
Pint of vellinvoyle.	*Pint of strong beer, please.*
Dylan Thomas Speshal.	*Bottle of whiskey and a pint mug.*
Yacky Dar.	*Cheers.*
Peaceful, Sunday.	*I was asleep in the sermon.*
Specially in Ceredigion (the Lleyn peninsula).	*Yes, rural Wales can be soporific.*
Owa bouta stroll after Chapel?	*Shall we go to the pub?*
Goin to look at them cattle, Olwen.	*We are going to the pub, wife.*
Mornin', Reverend.	*Good morning, Pastor.*
I am proceedin to my meditations.	*I am going for a walk.*

Round the garden . . .	*Creep round the side entrance . . .*
Where are the cattle?	*But it is closed Sundays.*
In the public bar, crretin bonce . . .	*Keep moving . . .*
Quick, through the door . . .	*Slither in . . .*
Stack em up, boyo.	*Ten pints, please.*
Down the atch!	*Cheers!*
Hello, Dai Beat!	*Morning, Constable.*
Hello again, Reverend.	*Hello again, Reverend.*
Yacky dar, boyobach.	*Cheers, my son.*

The Countryside

Twm lives down the cwm.	*Tom lives in the valley.*
Iss stip, look.	*The sides are precipitous.*
Up by the ditches.	*Near the hill fort.*
Beyond the Druid Stones.	*Beyond the megaliths.*
Ill farmer, Twm.	*Tom is eligible for EEC grants.*
You can't miss the farm.	*You will be lucky if you find the farm.*
It is the long ouse.	*House and barn are joined at their ends.*
Dright beside the tabernacle.	*Within a mile of the chapel.*
In the middle of the town.	*There are some other houses within a couple of miles.*
There is a little sea mist, intit?	*It is pouring with rain.*
Soon it will be fine.	*Later in the day, it may die away to a fine drizzle.*
Twm has a great farm.	*Tom has more than 100 acres.*
E as some pasture.	*He owns a mountain.*
E as some sheep pasture.	*He has a bare mountain.*

Ow green was my valley.	*Once, my valley was a haven of peace and industry.*

Ow black was my valley.	*Then my valley was severely polluted.*
Ow green my valley now.	*Now, nettles and brambles grow through the derelict mines and factories.*

Ladies and Gentlemen's Requisites

Jones Fish	*The fishmonger.*
Jones Fried Fish.	*The fish and chip shop.*
Jones Piranha Fish.	*The pet shop.*
Jones the Wad.	*The lucky amulet shop.*
Jones Death.	*The undertaker.*
Jones Fibber.	*The journalist.*
Jones Nitrogen.	*The farm supplies merchant.*
Jones Jelly.	*The Welsh Language Society.*
Giff me a dog, please.	*I would like to purchase a sheepdog.*
£100, £500, £1000.	*It is a poor sheepdog, a medium sheep dog, a fairly good sheepdog.*

I've a arp, look.	*I have just purchased a harp.*
I must buy a cattle from that kitchen shop.	*I require a kettle.*
Please sell me a cattle, Sam.	*A kettle, please, Sam.*
Please sell me a love spoon, a Welsh Dresser, an S4C.	*I need a wooden spoon, a kitchen unit, a TV channel.*
It is Drugby night.	*It is Thursday.*
Weer avin a discaw.	*A dance has been organised.*
There is very little fightin at this discaw.	*This is boring.*
Qme for me.	*I'm off.*
Wherrs your arp?	*Where's your harp?*
I left my arp in Sam Pans' Disco.	*Oh, dear.*

Taboos

Flood the Valleys.	*The Valleys have had their day and should be turned into reservoirs.*
Teach the lads from the pit to knit.	*Retrain the miners.*
Gif me Pam Ayers over an *englyn,* whatever.	*Welsh poetry is boring.*
Pards and Trewids? Cretins in bedsheets.	*Bards and druids look silly.*
Dreamed up by Iolo Morganoog, bards.	*Bards are a 19th century invention.*
English is good enough for me.	*The Welsh language is an irrelevance.*
Rugby Union is fun.	*Rugby Union is a sport.*

Bit like Rugby League, innit?	*Rugby Union is a debased form of Rugby League.*
I've got a new ouse in the Lleyn.	*I have just purchased a third home in North Wales.*
Plaid Cymru's Scottish.	*I thought Plaid Cymru was a sort of tartan.*
Don't Rover look appy, playin with the ship?	*Doesn't Rover look happy chewing that lamb?*

Country Cottage

Hellw.	*Hello.*
Sorry?	*I do not understand you.*
Ouse is bwrnin, look.	*My cottage is on fire.*
Dreely, now?	*How terrible.*
Oose callin?	*What is your name?*
Oliday visitor, is it?	*Do you have another address, in the Midlands say?*
1. No.	*No.*
Great. Engin's comin now.	*Help is on the way.*
2. Yes.	*Number 23 the Laurels, Solihull.*
Ah. Owmany kids, look?	*How many children do you have?*
Oh, they're fine, they're outside.	*Never mind the children. Please send the fire engine.*
Ave you ad smallpox?	*Have you had smallpox?*
We'll ave to see the certificates. Can't be too careful, look.	*I do not trust foreigners.*
The roooof . . .	*Please send the fire brigade.*
You wouldn't want the fire brigade to get oopin cough would you now?	*We do not trust foreigners.*
FOR GOD'S SAKE THE ROOF HAS FALLEN IN.	*Please send the fire brigade.*

There's good, then. Can't fall no further, can it?	*My task is nearly over.*
PLEEEASE!	*Please send the fire engine.*
Mind how you go, look.	*Goodbye, foreign devil.*

Wales — The W.I. Eisteddfod

Off we go, pal *bach.*	*Off we go, my little chum.*
To the *eisteddfod.*	*To the Culture Festival.*
Oo, Chrissmuss.	*I am not a culture buff.*
Ere's the Trewid!	*Here is a man in a white sheet.*
Why's he wearing that thing?	*Why does he have on a catering hat?*
Trewid's made an awdle.	*The man in the white sheet has written an ode.*
My bwm is nwmb.	*These benches are very hard.*
I can ear the shatters on the Grin Draggin.	*The pub has just closed.*
Enjoyin yourself, arr you?	*Suffer, English pig.*
I have hiraeth for a glass or two.	*I have a wistful longing for alcohol.*
Clap, clap.	*Thank goodness! Finished!*
Very nice, yes.	*Extremely boring.*
You'll enjoy the ssecond aff, then.	*The second half will be worse.*
Ssecond aff?	*Oh, no. Oh, no.*
Yess. Thiss iss only aff time, hee hee.	*I am twisting the knife.*
I ave a terrible pain in my leg.	*I am going.*
Tch, tch.	*The Welsh have never been defeated.*

Emergency Welsh

Elp!	*Help.*
Vee nahar a weddie torri lour.	*My car has just broken down.*
Blair mire cle agusaf e my guile petrol?	*Where is the nearest petrol station?*
Beth your ennoo er thle amma?	*What is the name of this place?*
Dangossook ee may achlair cle mire ti bach asgwillock anna tha.	*Please direct me to the toilets.*
Ble mire tavarn agassof (shop pissgod ac escloddin agasof)?	*Where is the nearest public house (fish and chip shop)?*
Adach cheean goobod a forrrd oddie ar a manaird heen?	*Do you know the way off this mountain?*
Pa foord an ol ear lan?	*Which way back to the shore?*
Roythe newedth weddie coompio oddie ar clogwin (manaird).	*I have just fallen off a cliff (mountain).*
Niddoif an please your ar cayedwadoor.	*I am not a tory voter.*
Nid vie mod weddie kyle nennie an syce (din tramore).	*I cannot help being English (foreign).*
Owen Glyndoor din predworth yawn.	*Owen Glendower very nice guy.*

MIDLANDS

Introduction

THE MIDLANDS ARE a mighty tapestry of rich colours nailed across the centre of England. They encompass the quiet colleges of Oxford, the post-industrial deserts of the West Midlands, the semi-barbarous hilltops of Shropshire, and the flat, shoe-bearing plains of Northants. At first sight, the linguistic variations of such a diverse topography might seem enormous. But language is a reflection of a state of mind, and it has been said that the Midlands are just that.

Life in the Midlands has never been easy. Those who have herded sheep in Salop, bashed metal in Birmingham or cobbled in Northants realise that these are solitary occupations which breed a hard commercial sense. Furthermore, the people of Midland cities did not separate their work and their homes, as in the longer-established South. Instead they tended to live over their workshops, at loggerheads with the neighbours for reasons commercial as well as domestic. Social and business rivalries were thus intertwined, and sweetness and light became rare as hen's teeth.

The inner-city workshops have largely vanished, and the lot of the shoemaker and farmer has improved. But the conversation of the Midlands is still rough, bloody-minded stuff, whether it is heard in the refined purlieus of Solihull or the franker Potteries.

There are various rules:

1) Be wily.
2) Never talk about people when you could be talking about cars.
3) Always talk about money.
4) Wear synthetic fibres next to the skin. The static electricity generated will keep you jumpy.

Pronunciation Note
Pronunciation is fairly straightforward. Try to intersperse remarks with a short, wise laugh, expressive of a belief in the impermanence of all things, especially husbands/wives, cars and development scheme units on industrial estates.

Travel

Ere! Yow!	*Excuse me!*
Wayer's Broom? (Wolverumpton, Coventroy)?	*Could you direct me to Birmingham (Wolverhampton, Coventry)?*
Whayer did yow git that huyp?	*Where did you get that dreadful car?*
Syme ployce yow got yower gob.	*Same place as you got your face.*
A sayd wayer's Broom?	*I was asking the way to Birmingham.*
Oopp thuy emm six . . .	*Up the M6 . . .*
threw the contryflow . . .	*through the contraflow system . . .*

pawst the foytal oxidant . . .	*past the fatal accident . . .*
up the bunk . . .	*up the hill . . .*
royt it the estoyt . . .	*right at the housing estate . . .*
lift at the indostreel pork . . .	*left at the for sale sign on the industrial park . . .*
stroyt ahed to the rowind corpork . . .	*follow your nose to the ruined car park . . .*
and yow'll soy the soyns . . .	*and you'll see the signs . . .*
ef yowre mowtor gets yow thet far.	*if your car survives the journey.*
Chuykoy bastod.	*Impudent person.*
Soddoff, plodd.	*I dispute that, officer.*

Thoyer's an eggzit.	*There's an exit.*
Ow. Inuther mowterwhy.	*Oh. Another motorway.*
Lowk! A sieuvices.	*Look! A services!*
Now, it's only a mowterwhy.	*No, it's only a motorway.*
Troy a lift.	*Try a left.*
Troy a royt.	*Try a right.*
Owlong a woy boyn hoyer?	*How long have we been here?*
Foyve menuts, foyve year.	*Five minutes, five years.*
Woyer trapped.	*We're trapped.*
Yer royt.	*You're right.*
Lowk! An eggzit.	*Look! An exit!*
Bludda es!	*It certainly is!*
Es ut Coventroy?	*Is it Coventry?*
Now, ut's Poybles.	*No, it's Peebles.*

Eating and Sleeping

Luke! A caff!	*Look! A restaurant!*
Ow, yeah.	*How splendid!*
A could fancey sum snap.	*I am eager for a snack.*

Cup a tay, ta . . .	*Cup of tea, please.*
Boykewell tart, styke an' kindypoy.	*Bakewell tart, steak and kidney pie.*
Bowel er lobby.	*Bowl of stew.*
Pencayk rowl, ta.	*Deep fried J cloth please.*
Fencey a styke?	*Would you like a steak?*
Ast patty de fwa gra?	*Do you have liver paste?*
No, I hanna.	*No, I have not.*
Yes, you ast.	*Yes, you have.*
Et's the bossiz.	*It is the manager's private supply.*
Gissabit, loike.	*I would like to fornicate with you.*
Gissa pawshun, loike.	*Could I have some paste, please?*
No, I dassna.	*I dare not give you any.*
A'll improwve the blodday showcase.	*I am about to use violence on your fixtures and fittings.*
Nooo, not with omma!	*Noo! Not with your hammer! Please . . .*
Luke, ay's bleedin!	*Look, he's bleeding!*
Not no mower, ay's bludda jed!	*Now he has stopped bleeding. He is dead.*
Off wom, then.	*Time to go home.*

Ey! Missis! Keny woy kip ere?	*Excuse me, madam, have you a bed for the night?*
Ef yow can pye.	*Certainly, sir.*
Fleppun ick! Bit owld, innit?	*Goodness. What an ancient, rundown, unfashionable-looking place!*
Norrasowld as yower motor.	*Not as ancient, rundown or unfashionable as your car.*

The Pub

Oy!	*Greetings, landlord!*
Yur.	*Good evening, gentlemen!*
Poynt a Bass.	*We are in the Midlands.*
Poynt a Springfoiled.	*We are in the West Midlands.*
Poynt a Flowers.	*We are in the South West Midlands.*
Poynt a Ansoles.	*We are somewhere in the Midlands.*
Choyers!	*Good health!*
Ow bista?	*How are you?*
Not tiew clever.	*Not well.*
Bludda comical.	*Not at all well.*
Oozat noyce bieud?	*Who is that attractive woman?*
Moy woyfe.	*My wife.*
Surrey, myte.	*Gosh. I am terribly sorry.*
Down't lit may stoppyer, ilp yoursilf.	*Not at all, go ahead.*
Gerroff.	*I believe your nonchalance is a pose.*
Shay's on the knock, allatime.	*She has many pounds of HP debts.*
Ow will then, ta but norrarowp.	*Well in that case, thank you but no thank you.*
Pass the fags around.	*Distribute cigarettes among the assembled company.*
Gorra loyt?	*Have you a light?*
Nowbodoy gorra metch?	*Has nobody a match?*
Anna anny onya anny onya?	*Haven't any of you any on you?*
Soddit.	*Bother.*
Mey for wom.	*I'm off.*

The Countryside, Industrial

Ear yow are, thin.	*We are now entering the Industrial Midlands.*
Ear's the Foyve Towens.	*Here is Stoke-on-Trent.*
Burrereze ownly won.	*But this is only one town.*
Roobish.	*Each segment of the ring road has its distinct characteristics.*
Luke! Ay doggey!	*Look! A mad Alsatian.*
Pore bastids.	*Look! A dole queue.*
A conna say the Blake Cuntra.	*Where is the Black Country?*
Ut lukes grain.	*It looks green.*
Ah, the fillers are owt (uts brock).	*Yes, there is a strike on (it is bankrupt).*
Ear's Wolverumpton, Kiddoy.	*Here are the industrial West Midlands.*
Wheer?	*Where are they?*
Owver wheer it siz FOW SAYL.	*Over there, with the For Sale sign on them.*
Ayst, now.	*Let us head east.*
Nuyd anny poys, shues?	*Do you require any pies or shoes?*
Wanna suy Miltin Keens?	*Shall we visit Milton Keynes?*
Nobluddeylikeloy.	*No.*
Ah.	*Wise, very wise.*
Ereze Burn.	*Here is Burton-on-Trent.*
Thoy myke Bass in Burn.	*Burton is the home of Bass Ale.*
Noyce ployce, Burn.	*What an impressive city.*
Gerris down yow.	*Let us linger a while.*

Ladies and Gentlemen's Requisites

Ezzat the milkman?	*Is that the milkman?*
Now, et's the Beer at Wom man.	*No, it's the Beer at Home man.*
Tirrif! Just in toyme for brikfist.	*Thank goodness! I was getting thirsty.*

I want sum clows.	*I would like to buy some clothes.*
Pear a shows.	*Pair of shoes.*
Jempi, shieut.	*A pullover, shirt.*
Neckers.	*Underpants.*
Pewer new ool?	*In wool?*
Now, twiip. Sinthitic foyber.	*Do me a favour. Bri-nylon, if available.*
Cloth cup en meck.	*Cloth cap and raincoat.*
Loyke a cloth cup en meck sit?	*Would sir consider a matching cloth cap and raincoat set?*

Now. Meck's tow smow.	*No, the raincoat does not brush my shoes.*
Lotta munoy.	*It is very expensive.*

Loike a viddyow, ta.	*Please give me a video tape.*
"Ow to ripeer yer Moystrow."	*"Mending your Maestro."*
"Fission for Grinmawstis."	*"Angling for Grand Masters."*
"Dwawf Cownifis for Expirs."	*"Dwarf Conifers for Experts."*
Grite.	*Thank you.*
Ow, won for the kiddoys . . .	*And one for the children . . .*
"Snow Whoyte and the Sivin Attachmints."	*"The Black and Decker Fairy Book."*

Taboos

Munoy is the rowt of all evyle.	*Money is the root of all evil.*
Bieumingum is oogloy.	*Birmingham is ugly.*
Stork is bowerin.	*Stoke-on-Trent is tedious.*
Miltin Keens? Wayerzat?	*I cannot find Milton Keynes.*
Telfid's yowseless.	*Telford will never be fully inhabited.*
Sowlihool's ay bitt loyke Dorking.	*Solihull aspires to be like Dorking.*
A nivver bothid with Northanton.	*I have never felt the need to go to Northampton.*
Yow'll all git yer caerds Thirsty.	*Redundancy notices will be issued on Thursday.*
Notts marnis is scubs.	*Nottinghamshire miners are strikebreakers.*
Brittis cors is roobish.	*British cars are lousy.*
Oy ayts indostreel arkillagy.	*Old factories should be demolished.*
Woyste of toyme, kinals.	*Old canals should be filled in.*

The Middlins is an indostreel reegin.	*The Midlands is an industrial region.*
The Middlins is a rowral reegin.	*The Midlands is a rural region.*

Brum Wily Talk

Ere! Yow!	*Excuse me!*
Ows the car?	*How are you, old chap?*
Ows that other car?	*How is your wife?*
Seen that milkman lately?	*How are your children?*
What bizniz is it of bloddy yours?	*Very well, thank you.*
Went to look at a nice car in Oxford todoy.	*I have been travelling abroad.*
Blowk in Oxford ask me for a loight for his cigar and I told him if he could afford cigars he could afford bloddy matchiz.	*Whilst abroad I met a rich man.*
Noice blowk.	*A thieving rogue.*
Noice blowk till he joined the police.	*A thieving rogue who has committed murder.*
Silly fowl lives near Kiddoy.	*A simple countryman.*
Did you see the tits on that barmaid? They're bloddy real, I powked 'em!	*The landlord has an attractive wife.*
Wait till the barmaid's blowk turns his beck and hittim with your car.	*The landlord is a large person of aggressive mien.*
Fancy a few drinks in Kiddoy?	*I think I need some country air.*

Trucker — The Language of the Motorways

Sod!	*Good day, fellow motorist.*
Sod cut me up.	*He has overtaken me.*

Seef wecan purrim over scent resvation.	*I am turning right.*
Seef wecan purrim over bankment.	*I am turning left.*
Fillerup, John.	*Please put diesel in my tank.*
Twennynicker differns, right?	*Please make my receipt out for £20 more than the diesel actually cost.*
Imer knight of the rowd.	*I am a tattooed yob.*
Arfnarf, kay.	*Both of us will profit from this move.*
Bleedin reefer.	*A refrigerated lorry.*
Bleedin artic.	*An articulated lorry.*
Coppler yorkis anna box a matchiz.	*Two Yorkies and a box of matches, please.*
But yount smowk.	*You don't smoke.*
Now, the matchiz is for me oys.	*No. The matches are to prop my eyelids open.*

The Rural Midlands — Polite Conversation

Ow bista?	*How are you?*
Pretty middlin.	*Well, thank you.*
Only middlin.	*Ill, thank you.*
But ornery.	*Very ill, thank you.*
It's arpast five wi' me.	*At death's door.*
Cor! E'm gone dyud!	*Heavens! He has passed Beyond!*

Bit fresh teday.	*The temperature is 0°F.*
Them's fixed it.	*Everything is frozen solid.*
I be starved o' cold.	*I am frozen.*
Bista gwin out, like?	*Are you going out?*
I expect so.	*Yes, definitely.*
I'm not sure.	*Certainly not.*

Day's gone ketchy.	*The weather has become unsettled.*
Day's gone dabbledy.	*The weather has become showery.*
Er's mizzling.	*It is drizzling.*
Er feels glemmy.	*Looks like thunder.*
Narsty wiffeldy wind.	*There's an aggravating breeze.*
Ar. Tis a lazy wind, goes stret thru 'ee.	*Yes. It is extremely cold.*
Bye for now.	*Au revoir.*
Bye.	*Adieu.*

Rural Midlands — The Hunting Field

Ah! There's hinds.	*Look! There are dogs, land-rovers, mounted gentlefolk and pedestrian vegetarians.*
Yes. Hullye, Cmilla (Hew, Annabel, Wollo). Nice nag!	*Greetings! That very large brown animal looks expensive!*
Hullye, Ashly, yes, *is* nice nag.	*Yes it was.*
O, there's Hew (Cmilla, Annabel, Wollo)!	*I am turning my back on you.*
Gud! A bluddy Anowak!	*Ugh! A vegetarian!*
Will sumbdy stup that bluddy little man? I say stuppim, stuppim!	*Would a strong person on a horse please whip the vegetarian?*
They're off!	*A vegetarian has spilt aniseed down his trousers and is making for the horizon hotly pursued by sixty dogs.*
Tally ho!	*There goes a fox (cat, rabbit, vegetarian)!*
Hark forrard!	*Someone somewhere is having a better time than we are.*

Gone away!	*The fox (cat, rabbit, vegetarian) has taken to its heels.*
Takin a dashd good line.	*The fox has spared us the necessity of jumping dangerous hedges.*
Gone to earth!	*The fox has bolted down a hole!*
Gave us a run for our money, tho' . . .	*Let us spare the noble quarry . . .*
Eaou. Here come the terriers.	*On second thoughts, let us dig it up and kill it.*
Tear 'im and eat 'im!	*Take this fox (cat, rabbit, vegetarian) and dispose of it, dogs.*

NORTH

Introduction

THE NORTH OF England is a region of fascinating diversity encompassing the high hills of Cumbria, the empty satanic mills of Manchester and a good deal in between. The one factor uniting the region is a deep mistrust of anyone from south of a line drawn from Liverpool to Lincoln, expressed by means ranging from violence at the one extreme to a clam-like reserve at the other. Politicians, closing down manufacturing industries for reasons not well understood by their victims, have tended to reinforce this basic mistrust. This may be why people who get on nicely in the North tend to be people who sound as little like the reigning species of politician as possible.

The Northern attitude is blunt, uncompromising, and admits of none of your hoity toity. This applies to the inanimate creation as well as to humans. Thus a

Northerner will call a spade a spade, but is equally likely (unless prevented by religious conviction) to call it a bloody spade. The influence of dour and monosyllabic Scandinavians has enriched the Northern vocabulary, particularly those parts of it dealing with dung and congenital idiocy. In the industrial areas, privation and factory smoke have added their ha'porths to the already gruff speech of the region. And in the high, lonely fastnesses of Cumbria and Northumbria, a mixture of inhospitable terrain and the constant presence of sheep has produced a pawky gloom approaching melancholy madness. Nowhere is a knowledge of regional idiom so important to the traveller for business or pleasure as in the North of England.

Pronunciation Note
Much Northern pronunciation is self-evident. *Diction* should be slow, precise and measured, since Northerners will only listen to you if you sound sensible. The *laugh* should be curt, nasal, and slightly scornful. There is nothing a Northerner dislikes as much as a vulgar display of inner feeling.

Travel

Ow do!	*Excuse me, sir or madam.*
Aye?	*What can I do to oblige?*
Tell ust roared for Wootherin Eyts?	*Please direct me to Wuthering Heights.*
Eyyy!	*Good heavens!*
A wudn't gan theer if a were thee!	*I think that is an unwise choice of destination.*
Art ont buz?	*Are you travelling by public transport?*
Nay, int caa.	*No, I am travelling by car.*
Gan throot yat . . .	*Go through the gate . . .*
swint feal wit beass . . .	*diagonally across the field with cattle . . .*

gan deeant roared pust mill.	*down the road past the mill.*
(There's trubble upt mill).	*(There are road works at the mill).*
They're alecking abowt wit drairns.	*New sewage works are in progress.*
Then ye mun tak t'fell roared.	*Follow the signpost to the hills.*
Champion!	*Excellent!*
Aye. Et's a dowly owd roared.	*Yes. It is a gloomy route.*
Pust t'gibbet and t'ungin tree.	*Past the gibbet and the blasted oak.*
Ye'll seet lodges.	*You'll see the gate lodges.*
Es ut sairf?	*Is it safe?*
Aye, if yer tak yer gaaluk necklet.	*Yes, provided you take your garlic necklace.*
Anna geates. Pust soomp . . .	*Anyway. Past the swamp . . .*
ye'll eart skrikin.	*and you'll hear the screams.*
Right taateh, Mister Eathcliff.	*Mr Heathcliff runs a tight health farm.*

Eating and Sleeping

Stupt caar (buz, trean)!	*Stop the car (bus, train)!*
Ah'm starved.	*I am very cold.*
A cud eat a poxy cow baht ketchoop.	*I am hungry.*
A be well meat yabble.	*I am very hungry.*
Reach to, mister and missus!	*Dig in, sir and madam!*
Fishen chips from Grimsba (Wiggin).	*Local fish and chips.*
Pust alicker.	*Pass the vinegar.*
Bleck peys! Greydla!	*Black peas! Excellent!*
Them chips's pleyed amlet wi me bowel.	*The chips have not agreed with me.*
Luke! Paakin!	*Look! Gingerbread!*

Winsladeal cheyas! Gormfleaks!	*Wensleydale cheese! Cornflakes!*
Ee, ah'm badli.	*I feel very ill.*
Gendle minkeak! Morcumbea srims!	*Kendal mint cake! Morecambe Bay shrimps!*
Ey, up. A feels right waffy.	*Dear me, I do feel weak.*
Me fort wooden ill.	*I must go upstairs.*
Can a kip ere, missus?	*Have you a bed for the night?*
Aye. Viewatilluminearshins.	*Yes, with a view of Blackpool Tower.*
Whassa ruckit?	*Is it not rather noisy?*
That'll be Doris wi coostomer.	*That must be the lady next door with another friend.*
Shall a buke thi in, dook?	*Would you like to meet her?*
Dust want piggy int bed?	*Would you like a hot water bottle?*
Nay, ta.	*Not tonight, thank you.*
Englis brekfist, ta.	*Black pudding, beans, eggs, chips, bread, mushrooms, tomatoes, please.*
Continental brekfist, ta.	*Black pudding fried in garlic, please.*

The Pub

Noo!	*Good evening landlord! What a wonderful day it has been!*
Noo, then!	*Indeed. And may I enquire what is your drinking pleasure?*
Paynt?	*We serve a full range of cocktails, but I suspect you prefer beer.*
Aye.	*A correct analysis of the situation. Most perspicacious.*

Nay.	*I am not convinced that I require such a large intake of liquid.*
Huf.	*I have therefore decided to order a mere half pint.*
Smiths.	*Smith's brewery has always seemed to produce a nutty, thirst-quenching product.*
Theakstons.	*While Theakstons Old Peculier has its appeal to those tired of standing on their hind legs.*
Broon.	*Newcastle Brown has carved a niche in my heart and duodenum.*
Seeamer gin.	*Perhaps you would be so good as to repeat my order?*
Baht andle, like.	*I prefer a thin glass constructed along the lines of a truncated cone.*
Sup up.	*Drain the flowing bowl, the better to refill it!*
By!	*Good heavens! I think I recognise that person.*
Ey, oop.	*Is your name by any chance Roger the Lodger?*
Ey, *oop*.	*How is my wife with whom you decamped last Thursday?*
Ey, oop.	*I think I will rend you asunder you oily little brute.*
Ey, oop.	*So! Flee if you will, we shall meet again.*
Yamfer me.	*It has been a tiring day. I shall return to my solitary bed.*
Ga neet.	*Farewell, fellow roisterers! Until our next brimming draught!*
Rubbit, bledda rubbit.	*What an exceptionally garrulous person.*

The Countryside

Int Range Roveh, luds!	*Let us go for a drive in the country.*
Ont Pennahn Weeah!	*Along the Pennine Way!*
Sa fear snazzlin marnen!	*A fine, crisp morning!*
Clarty owd roared.	*A muddy road.*
Mahnd that tup!	*Look out for that sheep!*
Mud a oppent yat?	*Shall I open the gate?*
Uppen tha wilt.	*Yes, Charles, I should be much obliged.*
Wheeah's Charlie?	*Charles has vanished.*
Int pot.	*He has fallen down a pothole.*
Ey, oop!	*The Range Rover has disappeared.*
It frames middlin bad.	*Things are not looking good.*
Dowly owd horl.	*That is a gloomy cave mouth.*
Cobble a steean in.	*Throw in a stone.*
Didsta year it lund?	*Did you hear it hit the bottom?*
Nay.	*I am afraid not.*
Theea's Range Roveh!	*I can see the Range Rover!*
Aye, an' Charlie!	*I can see Charles!*
Range Roveh's med sad deed o' Charlie.	*The Range Rover has fallen on top of Charles.*
Ello, umblins?	*Ambulance, please.*
Range Roveh's at bottom o' Geapin Gill.	*I would like to report a Range Rover at the bottom of Gaping Gill.*
Wid best gan yam.	*We had better go home.*

Ladies and Gentlemen's Requisites

Ad lak sum ship.	*Please may I have some sheep?*
Ow manny ship?	*How many sheep?*
Yan, tyan, tethera, methera, pimp, sethera, levera, hovera, dovera, dick ship.	*One, two, three, four, five, six, seven, eight, nine, ten sheep.*
Astat brass?	*Have you the money?*
Aye, that I ave.	*Yes I have.*
Takt ship, then.	*Then you may have your sheep.*

Giss a pow.	*Cut my hair, please.*
Blor drei? Kegs?	*Blow dry? Curlers?*
Nay, regler pow.	*No, an ordinary haircut.*
Ey, up! Gerrim!	*Hoy! There he goes!*
Girrimt pow-slap!	*Slap him viciously on the nape!*
Aargh!	*Ouch! That hurt!*

Me tranni's brork.	*My radio doesn't work.*
Owmooch te fixut?	*How much to mend it?*
Quid nooat, like.	*One pound.*
Gie ower! That's dear-like.	*Goodness! How expensive!*
Gitta boonch, en.	*Give it a kick, then.*
Mean as muck.	*You are certainly a parsimonious person.*

Nobbut yan.	*Only one.*
A poorish few.	*Not many.*
A middlinish few.	*Several.*
A good few.	*Lots.*
A canny few.	*An enormous quantity.*

Taboos

Lancasheer? Bint that in Yorksheer?	*Lancashire is part of Yorkshire.*
Tane en Weeah's in Yirkshi.	*So is Newcastle.*
Lotti Toris in Doorim.	*Durham is solidly behind Mrs Thatcher.*
Ye're orreight, a grant ye, boot reel min coom fra Surrey.	*Real men come from the South.*
Yal's piss.	*I don't like beer.*
There's nowt so queer as folk.	*Folk music is for homosexuals only.*
Yorksheer folk taak ower much.	*Yorkshire people are over-garrulous.*
Jeffra Boykit's a daft twerp.	*Geoffrey Boycott is a devil.*
Jeffra Boykit's a bledda yeero.	*Geoffrey Boycott is an angel.*
Am a bessbawl man masen.	*Personally I prefer rounders to cricket.*
A mek meates right fast, me.	*I believe in love at first sight.*
Ah've spit in yer yal.	*I have spat in your beer.*

General Bluntness

Thee wit flat face!	*You with the small features!*
Nay, t'oother won! Wit big gob!	*No, not you! The one with the large mouth.*
What do they call thee?	*What's your name?*
Tha mun be right dense.	*You must be very stupid.*
Tha's dribbled tha grub.	*You have spilt your food down your front.*
Yon's no dribble, yon's ma new tie.	*You are speaking of my new tie.*
Ye gormless twerp.	*Idiot!*

What bloddy novice bout that car?	*What fool bought that car?*
Ah'll doer oop.	*Me, in order to restore it.*
What, a gret neverswet lak thee?	*What, a lazy person like you?*
Yonderish berk.	*You have ideas above your station.*
Tha gert, sackless, headed fule, tha!	*Moron!*
Hod thi clack, wench!	*Silence, wife!*
Thart bledda youseless!	*Good for nothing!*
Comin upt pub, lad?	*Fancy a pint, my son?*
Ay, dad, that I um.	*Yes, dad.*

Geordie

Ow there, marra!	*Hello, dear friend!*
What cheer, hinny?	*Hello yourself, old pal!*
Wheer ya gannin?	*Where are you going?*

To the offeece.	*To the office.*
Are ye gannin to walk?	*Are you going to work?*
Nay, I'm gannin to work.	*No, I am going to walk.*
Hoo ya gannin?	*How will you travel?*
Onna metroar.	*On the Metro.*
Come thy ways.	*Come along, then.*
Why aye!	*I believe I will!*
Comebye, you!	*Excuse me, please.*
Tell us the wee to Heemorkit, me canny man!	*Please direct us to Haymarket, kind sir.*
Nooa, ye dafty.	*No, you foolish person.*
Divvent argy, but!	*Don't argue!*
Haad on!	*Hold tight!*
Hadaway and shite!	*Bother and blow!*
Ah'm doon!	*I have fallen over!*
Tek a tab, mon.	*Have a cigarette, pal.*
Nay, ta, ah'm scumfished.	*No thanks, my lungs will not stand it.*
Noo ah'm hacky dorty.	*Now I'm filthy dirty.*
Ower let for walk.	*Late for work.*
Ah'm gannin t'oil me wig.	*I'm off for a drink or two.*
Fancy a jill?	*Fancy a half?*
Aye.	*Yes.*

Entertainment — The Working Man's Club

48 pahnce, ta.	*Forty eight pints please.*
Soop oop, lads!	*Drink hearty!*
Ere's vorclist.	*Here is the singer.*
Fantastic sin ger.	*Very talented vocalist.*
Nayce joogs.	*Pleasant bosom she has.*
Smallern (biggern) our Ena's.	*She reminds me of my sister.*
That wer gret.	*Intermission.*

A mun empty mi clog.	*I must visit the toilet.*
Ey, oop, ere cumst comic.	*Now it is the comedian's turn.*
Luke at that twat!	*Look at that idiot!*
Nippin about cobby as owt!	*Hopping around merry as a grig!*
E's bahn dee.	*Time to fix him.*
GERROFF.	*We do not like you.*
ON YER BAHK.	*We do not like that joke.*
GIM A WIGGIN KISS SOMBADDA.	*Butt him in the face, someone!*
THART NOWT ATS OWT.	*Entertainment wise, you are a big zero.*
Nay, is thropple's badli.	*Give him a chance, he has a sore throat.*
Norras badlizinaminnit.	*Not as sore as it soon will be.*
Wet while 'e stops.	*Wait till he finishes.*
Champion!	*He has stopped.*
That were revoltin.	*He was not a success.*
Ey, a do lak a comic.	*How I love listening to comedians.*

Liverpool — An Evening Out

Cum 'ead!	*Come on!*
Orright la.	*All right.*
Gna duwit owver, know wharrameyn?	*We are about to commit Breaking and Entering.*
Burrits the blurra Gardin Isibishun.	*But it's the Garden Exhibition.*
Cufteeria. Dig in!	*Here's the cafeteria. A table!*
Coosty scran, eh?	*Excellent food, is it not?*
Ay, sound.	*Yes, very good.*
Creyp owva tow the cownteh . . .	*Creep across to the bar . . .*

ave sum bevvies.	*get some drinks.*
Ye luke right made up.	*You look very happy.*
Anything in the till?	*Anything in the till?*
Few greenies and a flim.	*Some pound notes and fiver.*
Whassamarrer?	*What is it?*
Buzies!	*Cheese it, the cops!*
Cum off it!	*Nah!*
O I yeah!	*Yes really!*
R. Ay!	*Oh, no!*
Out the jigger!	*Down the alley at the back.*
Me kecks has fell down.	*My trousers have fallen down.*
They're all around the danny.	*The car is surrounded.*
Blood yell.	*It's a fair cop.*

Isle of Man — The Business Meeting

Good dee.	*Good morning.*
I have a little achlish.	*I have a little bundle under my arm.*
You'd be from across?	*Are you from the mainland?*
I would.	*Yes.*
Augh-augh!	*Dear me!*
Capers, man, capers!	*Someone has been playing little games!*
Yon accountant's a clether.	*This accountant is not strictly honest.*
I am he.	*I am that accountant.*
Mphm.	*In that case, please accept my congratulations.*
Wheer's the sheerholders munoy?	*Where are the profits?*
The Mob's gottum.	*The fairies walked off with them.*

They're in me pick.	*They are in my Cayman Islands stash.*
I'm a shlute feller.	*I am a cunning operator.*
I have a slope staff.	*I employ crafty people.*
We'll get sorted middlin handy.	*We shall shortly achieve a happy outcome.*
Put the lawlums on the Eye Are Ess.	*Put the mockers on the Revenue.*
Threap as they wull.	*Kick and scream though they may.*
We'll give 'em a lie with the lid on.	*We will present them with a water tight case.*
Pop.	*I have unlidded the Bollinger.*
Come, break the straw.	*Here's to a long and profitable association.*

An Evening's Sport

Great naht out at rec.	*There is an evening of entertainment at the Recreation Ground.*
Dog, darts, pigeons an' Rugba.	*Whippet racing, darts championships, pigeon racing and Rugby League.*
There ghost oota.	*The timekeeper has blown the steam whistle.*
Ooz lads is winnin!	*Our side is winning!*
Dog's dahved into pack.	*A whippet has leapt into the scrum!*
Gim a earla buth!	*Send that whippet off, ref!*
Oo threw that arra?	*Who threw that dart?*
Scroom uf's blurra trunsfixed.	*The scrum half has been pierced.*
E's running 2,200 feet per min fort dressin room.	*He is running for the dressing room at 25 mph.*

T'winger's tackled me pigeon! — *The winger has tackled a pigeon!*

T'pigeon adn't possession! — *The pigeon was not holding the ball!*

Send bugger off! — *Send him off!*

Gim a thood, ref! — *Hit that pigeon fancier, ref!*

T'feavert's bit ref! — *The favourite has bitten the referee!*

Ere cumt forwards! — *Here come members of the scrum!*

Feace shoovla, an a tag team! — *In their private lives they are a human JCB and an all-in wrestling duo.*

Ee! Can't luke! — *What an appalling spectacle!*

There goat fanciers! — *The pigeon fanciers are beating a retreat.*

There goat dogs . . . nay . . . — *So are the whippets . . . no . . .*

Fullback's cheasint lead dog . . . — *The fullback is approaching the finishing line a nose behind the lead whippet . . .*

Eal a arras . . . — *in a hail of darts . . .*

Fullback'st winna! — *The full-back wins!*

Peayin nobbut 6-5. — *But the price was only six to five.*

SCOTLAND

Introduction

The culture of Scotland is as different from that of the rest of Britain as haggis from pork sausages. Scots have their own laws, their own customs, their own folklore. They may view the English with some suspicion. This is not surprising when you consider that the English, having spent the best part of four hundred years subduing them, now seem to be doing their best to cut them adrift, having first looted everything not actually a geographical feature (except oil wells). It is a tribute to the hospitable instincts of the Scots that English tourists are seldom found floating face downward in Loch Lomond.

The conventional image of the Scot, as a kilted figure jingling two bawbees furtively in his sporran, has changed. The new Scot is seen as a fiercely bearded figure three-quarters full of MacEwan's lager and topped up with hoarse cries about football teams. Neither of these is representative. In fact, the average foreigner is often shocked to find that at first glance the Scots are exactly like the inhabitants of the rest of Britain. The shock deepens when he finds that his first impression was disastrously wrong, and that when he is in Scotland he is Abroad.

Abide by local customs. If possible, find a real Scot to show you round. And whatever you do, resist the temptation to patronise. You may think that you are in a cold, wet country more suited to mountain goats and aeroplanes than human beings. The natives think otherwise.

Pronunciation Note
There is no harm in imitating a Scottish accent if you feel like it. Always pronounce "ch" as in "lechayim."

Travel

Hoots mon!	*I am a tourist.*
Aye?	*Can I be of assistance?*
Wheer's Glesga (Orban, Feef, Lairgs)?	*Please direct me to Glasgow (Oban, Fife, Largs).*
A dinna ken.	*I do not wish to speak today.*
A ken fu'weel.	*I know the way.*
Sput ut oot, mon.	*Please share your knowledge.*
Ye'll gang stracht aheid . . .	*Go straight on . . .*
ye'll tairn leeft fornenst the kirk . . .	*turn left past the church . . .*
ye'll tairn recht aneth the aik . . .	*turn right under the oak . . .*
and ye'll scoot through the doup o' the cleuch.	*and go through the bottom of the ravine.*
Mind ye dinna get lairt.	*Mind you don't get bogged down.*

It's sair dubby anent the scaur.	*It is very muddy opposite the clearing.*
Then ye'll be on the hill road . . .	*Then you are on the road across the mountains . . .*
Tis an oonchancie road . . .	*It is an uncanny spot . . .*
Aye, it's weel kent . . .	*Well known to be . . .*
If ye're theer at the darkenin . . .	*If you are there at dusk . . .*
ye'll see Weird Wullie . . .	*you will see Weird William.*
There's a mony that's foonert in the drift . . .	*Several people have broken down in the blowing snow . . .*
and Wullie's come tae ilka yin.	*and each time Willie has appeared.*
A weird gangrel . . .	*He is a ghastly wanderer . . .*
dreist in yaller.	*dressed all in yellow.*
Aye, ut's a dowie dee if ye're no signit up when Wullie comes by.	*It is a sad day for non AA members when Willie comes by.*

The Pub

Am gizzened wi'drooth.	*I am parched.*
Weel, ye'd best slock it.	*Pour beer on it, then.*
Am gauny boozer.	*I am going to the pub.*
Naw, ut's the Sabbath.	*No, it is Sunday.*
Aw, weel, am gauny hootale.	*In that case, I am going to the hotel.*
Gissa dram.	*I would like some whisky.*
Gissa peent a heavy.	*Pint of bitter, please.*
Gissa wee heavy.	*Strong ale, please.*
Wull ye come cairtin?	*Do you want to play cards?*
Deil-a-fears, mon.	*Not bleeding likely.*
Am for a guid doonsittin'.	*I have things to drink about.*

Greet crood here the streen.	*There were a lot of people here last night.*
Aye, an amony on 'em stull heer.	*Yes, and a lot of them are still here.*
Awa toe yer porridge, ye swines!	*Go to your breakfasts!*
Ye'll tak a dram?	*Will you have a glass of whisky?*
A hauf.	*Just a half of bitter.*
Uts the nee opening.	*It is the new opening times.*
They're here aw neet.	*I am full of customers on a round the clock basis.*
Am deen.	*I think I am dying with exhaustion.*

Eating and Sleeping

Lates git a carry-oot.	*Shall we get a takeaway meal?*
Late's gang dooni carfi.	*Let's go to the restaurant.*
Ereza wifie.	*There is the lady proprietor.*
Hulloooo!	*Excuse me, madam!*
Port a tea.	*Pot of tea, please.*
Oot barnocks wi' butter.	*Oatcakes with butter.*
Ad leek sugar wi' ma porridge.	*I am an effeminate foreigner.*
Drap on a wee scrappie ream.	*Put on some cream.*
Yon's a scrunt wee chaft.	*That is a chop of restricted growth.*
Yon's braxy.	*That meat died of natural causes.*
Finnan haddies! Brulliant!	*I like smoked haddock.*
Ad leek a steek.	*Please may I have a steak.*
Weel done.	*Cooked through.*
Gey reer.	*Fairly rare.*
Unco reer.	*Very rare.*

Bluidy.	*Still hot from the slaughter.*
Them's killer neeps!	*Those are excellent turnips!*
Aye, greeat kail.	*Yes, the food is excellent.*

Wull we gang up the stair?	*Come upstairs.*
Hoo does the heatin wurk?	*How does the heating work?*
The heatin's me.	*I am the heating.*

The Countryside

Awa' we gang.	*We're off!*
A grand wee promenade on the hull!	*A very long and mountainous walk.*
A have ma baps in ma sporran.	*I have brought a packed lunch.*
Noo we're comin' through the rye.	*We are tramping across standing corn.*
To the banks and braes . . .	*We are in the foothills . . .*
then the lin and whin-bushes . . .	*then in the heather and gorse . . .*
a wee bit moss . . .	*a bottomless swamp . . .*
A'm fear drookit, mon.	*I'm soaked!*
A'm forefochen.	*I'm exhausted!*
Cease girnin', chiel!	*Stop whining, weakling!*
Hark tae the whaups wheepin!	*Listen to the curlews whistling!*
See the stirks on the haugh below!	*Look at the bullocks far below by the river.*
A wee dram, wi' burn wechter.	*A gulp of whisky with water from the stream.*
And awa' tae the lochan in the corrie.	*And off to the little lake under the ridge.*
Grand country, grand country!	*Nightmarish crags loom on all sides.*
Luke! Ower the seas tae Skye.	*On a clear day you can see forever.*

Charlie is ma darlin . . .	*My boyfriend's name is Charles.*
But ye'll dae.	*But you are an acceptable substitute.*
Lanely here on the wee hull.	*It is lonely here on top of Ben Nevis.*
Naewheer tae rin, forebye . . .	*Besides, you could not run away, even if you wanted to . . .*
The scree, mon, the scree!	*No, not down that precipice of tumbled stone!*
A wheer tell me wheer has ma hielan' laddie gone?	*Where is that pretty young man?*
How can ye chant, ye little birds And I sae weary fu'o' care?	*It is a long walk home.*

Ladies and Gentlemen's Requisites

Ad leek a cork.	*I would like a rooster.*
Nae corks.	*We are out of roosters.*
Hoos yer hins?	*How are you off for hens?*
Nae hins.	*We are out of hens.*
Foo's yer doos?	*How are your pigeons?*
Aye pickin.	*Still taking nourishment.*

Ad leek a kult.	*I should like a kilt.*
That yin's ower lang.	*This one comes down to my ankles.*
That yin's ower shirt.	*This one arrives at mid-thigh.*
That yin's gey guid.	*This one touches the ground when I kneel and is therefore correct.*
Which plaid?	*Which tartan does sir require?*
A dinna guv a fug.	*Doesn't matter.*
But . . . but . . .	*I am shocked.*

Yon's pirty.	*Oh, very well. That one's pretty.*
Aye. 'Tis the Huntin Rubinstein.	*Yes. Lemon yellow with shocking pink stripes.*
Tis the Royal Abdullah.	*This tartan was worn by the Black Prince.*

Taboos

Tuppacle Scotsman? Weel, there's Harry Lauder.	*Harry Lauder is my idea of a Scotsman.*
Ut's a braw bricht moonlich nicht the nicht.	*I am trying to be funny.*
Whut de ye weer unner yon thing?	*What do you wear under your kilt?*
Nairth Sea Ile's a British arset.	*North Sea Oil belongs to the English.*
Gallic's deid.	*Scottish Gaelic is a dead language.*
Naebuddy wanted devolution.	*Self-government was extremely unpopular.*
Scorts Law? Pshaw!	*Scottish Law is an irrelevance.*
The Hebrides cannae support leef.	*The Islands are unfit for human habitation.*
A dinnae give a damn which kirk agouti.	*I am an ecumenical person.*
Gauf's a gemme fer lassies.	*Golfers are effeminate.*
Gauf's a gemme.	*Golf is a game.*
Fitba? Boorin.	*Football is boring.*
Rangers are margic.	*Rangers are excellent.*
Celtic are margic.	*Celtic are excellent.*
A leek a wee drappie Ribena in ma malt.	*Ribena enhances the taste of malt whisky.*

Camping

Yon's a seet!	*There's a camping site!*
What a bonny seet!	*What an attractive one!*
Harndy for the netty!	*Close to the toilets!*
Queet a vesta!	*Some view, too!*
I'll gang reygister the noo.	*I'll go and register.*
The nam's Campbell.	*My name is Campbell.*
Oh, aye.	*Really?*
Three quid, ta.	*Three pounds please.*
Leets oot.	*Let's turn out the lights.*
Aye, me for the beid.	*Yes, I am tired.*
What's yon raikit?	*What's that noise?*
A dinna ken.	*I don't know.*
Shit yer een, wife.	*Go to sleep, woman.*

Yon raikit's gey lood.	*That noise is pretty loud.*
AAAARCH!	*AAAARGH!*
O gard this is turble.	*As an American I find this depressing.*
Nam, addrais, dreivin leecence.	*Papers, please.*
Ochone! Deid, a'deid!	*Alas! Three killed in campsite horror!*
Gie's yer nam, a seid.	*Name, please.*
Ma nam's Macdonald.	*I am called Macdonald.*
Gie's yer hand.	*Let me shake you by the hand.*
Wheer am a?	*What is the name of this place?*
Glencoe Visitor Centre.	*The Glencoe Visitor Centre.*

Industrial Regeneration

Whu's yon nip?	*Who is that Japanese person?*
Hello, Tojo.	*Good afternoon, Mr Funicula.*
Gie's some ships.	*I wish some chips, please.*
Rarpud dalivera.	*Quick delivery.*
Hoo mony ton?	*How big?*
Aboot feeve.	*Five tons.*
Ye disappeent ma.	*That is smaller than I had hoped.*
A dinnae want ships, a want ships.	*I don't want ships, I want chips.*
Ships, ya tube.	*Chips, moron.*
Weel, we're no greet fryers here.	*We are not experienced chip fryers.*
The wains must eat, but . . .	*But our children must eat . . .*
We'll turn oor haun to't, Tojo.	*and we are hard hit by the recession.*

Teel us what ye need, ma wee gookie.	*So what is it you require, Slanteyes?*
Three meelion a these be Tuesda.	*Three million of these in a week.*
Ye'd need a midget tae whaled one a them.	*But we have no welding equipment suitable.*

Oil City

Will ya luke at that!	*Look at that!*
Luke a'wha?	*Look at what?*
Yon quine.	*That young lady.*
Yon quine wi'yon glaikit loon?	*The one with the weedy-looking bloke?*
Na. Yon quine wi' the greet geology.	*No. The promising-looking one.*
Oh, aye.	*You think so?*
Am a toolpusher.	*Good evening. I am a rich oilrig operative.*
A'm off.	*I am on leave.*
Camintae the cair pairk, noo.	*Come for a stroll in the granite moonlight.*
Oh! Ye're spuddin' in already?	*You have commenced drilling?*
Will ye never leave off stubbin?	*You are certainly committing quantities of equipment to this well.*
Yon's a tremenjous derrick.	*The equipment is of high quality.*
Yer well's no sae bad.	*So is the well.*
Ach, goad, a'm shot firin'.	*Seismic activity is being checked.*
Gone critical.	*I feel we will shortly strike oil.*
Blow-oot!	*Bingo!*
Oh.	*Well.*

Oh, aye.	*Yes, well.*
See's a fag, wullya?	*Could I please have a cigarette?*

The Distillery Visit

Helloo!	*Welcome to the Auld Bletherum Distillery.*
Yon's the malting floor.	*We are in a hot shed full of wet barley.*
Noot the peat reek.	*The air is full of choking peat smoke.*
Here the bairley's stairch becams sigar.	*Here enzymes turn the starches into sugars.*
A mun tak a pee.	*Having whipped the key from the guide's pocket, I am off to lock myself in the hospitality suite.*
Oh, aye.	*I do not have your initiative, fellow tourist.*
Luke a' the malt, noo.	*This is what the malt looks like.*
Rivetin'.	*I cannot wait to get to the hospitality suite.*
Yon's the mash tun.	*Malt is boiled in that huge vat.*
Ah, aye.	*How long till we get to the hospitality suite?*
Yon's the wash backs.	*This mighty cylinder is where the liquid ferments.*
Ecch, aye.	*What a disgusting smell. How long till we get to the hospitality suite?*
Loo wines come oot o' the wash still.	*The first fermentation produces a raw, crude spirit.*
Oh, aye.	*The hospitality suite, ta.*
And heer's the sperrut seef.	*This is where the finished whisky emerges.*

Oh?	*Do you know the combination?*
And the barrelin' plant.	*And is put into oak barrels for its long sleep.*
Ah!	*Now we are getting close to the hospitality suite!*
Will ye tak a dram, noo?	*I expect you would like a to taste our whisky.*
Oh, aye!	*Werl, if you insist.*
Dearie me, the key's gone!	*Alas, it seems we are locked out.*
Ochone!	*Oh, dear.*

Non-verbal Communication

Och.	*Oh.*
Hmm.	*I am considering your request.*
Mphm.	*I have heard what you say and am forced to agree.*
Ssss!	*I disagree.*
Tch!	*I disagree sharply.*
Hic!	*I am a little intoxicated.*
Ugh!	*I find that disgusting.*
Aaaah.	*That gives me pleasure.*
Eeee.	*I am still considering your request.*
EEEEEEE!	*I have just seen the Loch Ness Monster.*
Phew!	*The Loch Ness Monster has swum away.*

Emergency Gaelic

Coer!	*Help!*
Chair mee ashach.	*I have missed the ferry.*

Vel lyepi ackiv?	*Have you a bed for the night?*
Ham fishge bether sho' wadjer!	*The whisky is very strong.*
Care an ty beg?	*Where is the toilet?*
Chaimy lesh a crake.	*I have fallen off a cliff.*
Vel coer a yee vist?	*Do you need help?*
Hatto why me air aroon harst.	*No, I have not yet landed.*

IRISH SUPPLEMENT

Introduction

THE ENGLISH VIEW of Ireland is a collection of clichés, many of them linguistic. The reason that the English have hung on to their miserable preconceptions is that the Irish combine a massive tolerance of foreigners with the best manners in Europe. Much of Irish English is devoted to making the best of chains of events which tend towards decay, ruin and disintegration. This is a mental discipline alien to most Englishmen, members as they are of the rudest nation in Europe.

An Irish professor, at a conference in Spain, was asked by a Spaniard colleague if there was a word in Ireland corresponding to the Spanish *mañana.* The Irishman pondered deeply, and then replied that as far as he knew there was nothing that expressed such a degree of urgency. English and American visitors quickly discovered the truth of this remark, known to the patronising as the Catholic

Conception of Time. Victims are easy to spot. They are the ones hooting frantically in the traffic jam, or blundering round the unstaffed post office screaming with rage and frustration, while the native population politely averts its eyes.

Finally, Ireland is a nation of individuals. Your shop assistant may easily be descended from kings, and your managing director from gunmen. So never boss anyone about. Advanced Irish-English speakers present questions as a challenge. The bald 'Give me a packet of biscuits, please,' implies that the vendor is a sort of robot, there only to be of service to customers. If you phrase it: 'You wouldn't ever have a packet of biscuits?' however, the vendor can bask in the customer's incredulity that he should have had the high intelligence and powerful business acumen to lay in the Digestives against just such an eventuality.

Ireland is a topic which repays long study, and these three points merely skim the surface. Fieldwork is essential.

Pronunciation

Forget Terry Wogan and Paddy McGinty's goat. Most Irishmen and women speak with a tremendous purity.

Travel

Jasus will you look at the clouds on them hills!	*We are arriving in Ireland.*
Now there's a man having a bad day.	*Surely the driver of that car is intoxicated?*
It is the will of God.	*This is intolerable.*
Sure, it is a grand thing the infrastructure.	*The road is being repaired, it seems.*
The infrastructure will always give yez fierce jobs.	*The road has been being repaired for five years.*

The lads is after shooting the signpost to bits Satda.	*There seems to be no signpost.*
The lads is after givin the signpost a twist.	*The signpost says turn left for Cork.*
Tis a grand place to spend the night.	*We are lost.*
It is the will of God.	*The hire car is erupting.*
Looky for us the bus is runnin' spot on a week late.	*What a marvellous bus service!*
The yoke was banjaxed entirely. It was the will of God.	*I fear we shall need another car, the first one you hired us having become unserviceable.*
Would ye ever tell us where's the earport?	*Do you know where the airport is?*
Sure you'll take the first left, second right and it'll be plain as the nose on yer face.	*I do not know where the airport is.*
I am after falling out of a class of a small door on to the runway.	*Where is the lavatory on this aircraft?*

Eating and Sleeping

God th'owd beg's fleppin.	*My stomach thinks my throat is cut.*
Ye wouldn't ever have anny fish, now?	*Have you got fish?*
I would.	*Yes.*
I have whate trout, fluke . . .	*Sea trout, flatfish . . .*
smork sarmin, sarmin steek . . .	*smoked salmon, salmon steak . . .*
Bords eye fush fengers.	*Bird's Eye Fish Fingers.*
Hev ye be anny chents anny vidgertables?	*Have you got any vegetables?*
I hev	*Yes.*

I hev cabbage and spoods.	*We've got cabbage and potatoes.*
Would ye mek us a fray, missis?	*Madam, please give me a plate of sausages, eggs, bacon, pork, Kerry venison etc.*
Wit extry reshers?	*With extra bacon?*
Beck to the bid, now.	*An excellent late snack.*

Hev ye a bid?	*Have you accommodation for the night?*
Ad say a hiv.	*This converted barracks has 412 bedrooms and I can't remember which one is occupied.*
What is thet drippin?	*There is an odd noise.*
It is the tenk aboov on the joyces.	*It is the roof tank.*
What is thet roarin?	*What is that noise?*
It is the missis roaring.	*It is my wife weeping.*
The tenk above is after plommetin.	*The roof tank has come on to our bed.*
It is a tarpoleon you'll be needin.	*This tarpaulin might come in handy.*
It is the will of God.	*What do you expect, if you stay in a hotel?*

The Pub

A poob!	*Look! A pub!*
Wheer?	*Where?*
Thayer! And thayer! And thayer!	*There are five in the main street and one each in the grocer's shop, the ironmonger's, the funeral parlour, and the public library.*

How do?	*Good morning, customers.*
Gless of Guinnus (Murphy, Beamish).	*Half of stout, please.*
Paint of Hairp.	*Pint of lager, please.*
Half of Peddy.	*A large whiskey, please.*
Gless of Peddy.	*A very large whiskey, please.*
I am sober.	*I have had about a pint.*
I am after hevin drink teaken.	*I am drunkish.*
I am dhroonk.	*I am fairly intoxicated.*
I am meggoty dhroonk.	*I am drunk and about to perform an amazing feat of driving.*
I am jarred.	*I am semi-conscious or worse, and on the point of getting political.*
The reckit inside in the beck is the Pioneers.	*That drunken singing is the Temperance Association AGM.*
Here's the TD!	*Here is the local Member of of Parliament.*
He dooz heve a wonderful floo of talk.	*He can speak for many days without stopping.*
Good look!	*Goodbye!*

The Countryside

I'm lookin for the tatched house.	*I am searching for my holiday cottage.*
Ah! Ye'll be wantin Ballydereenkilsaggartmore!	*I had already guessed.*
Tes a feer saze town.	*There are three cottages there.*
Turn left, op the boreen.	*Turn left up the cart track.*
Tes a grand lettle house.	*What a pretty cottage!*

There dooz be a jacks beyond in the slob . . .
There is a privy in the swamp . . .

thin a ditch . . .
then a hedge . . .

amd a feer fairm of lend.
and a few acres of pasture.

Ye hev a grand strand view . . .
There is a fine view of the beach . . .

wit messive rowins . . .
and several wonderful ruins . . .

There is a kestle beloa . . .
a castle down there . . .

Cramwell knacked ut. . .
Cromwell destroyed it. . .

and the Beg House beyond . . .
and a large Georgian House.

Yer man is efter floggin the trees.
The new owner has cut down the 500 year old oaks and sold them.

He is efter floggin the house for hardcore.
He has pulled down the Palladian wing and sold it for road stone.

Bot he's a canserveationist.	*He has found it impossible to canalise the river.*
The leds borned ut in the Bed Time.	*The IRA burned it in 1922.*
The hoase is demp.	*The house is not very dry.*
Sure tes reanin.	*But of course it's raining.*
Sure tes a bit softish.	*But of course it's drizzling.*
Sure tes a grand dea.	*It is either raining, drizzling or the sun is shining.*
Tes a grand dea altogether.	*The sun is shining.*
Tes a hardy dea.	*It is raw and blustering, but the sky is blue.*
Tes a great plearce altogether.	*While the cottage is a ruin, the play of the clouds on the valley is a miracle.*
Ye're welcome here.	*We are genuinely glad you came.*

Ladies and Gentlemen's Requisites

Helloa!	*Good morning.*
Tes a grand dea.	*The sun rose this morning.*
Air ye will?	*I trust you are in good health.*
Hood'ye fencer for the Arl Airland?	*Which team will win the Hurling Championships?*
Hev yez a harse for the 2,000 Guineas?	*Have you a racing tip?*
Terrible time they do be havin below in Africa.	*World politics give cause for concern.*
I want wan of them yokes.	*I would like one of them.*
What cless of a yoke de ye want?	*What exactly did you want?*
A cless of a yoke you wad pale a spod wit.	*A potato peeler.*

This cless of a yoke?	*This mechanised hay rake?*
More of a knafe cless of a yoke.	*No, a knife would be better.*
Raight, so.	*Quite.*

Taboos

The Celts did be livin in the mod hots.	*Celtic Civilisation is a myth.*
Cramwell, now. There was a man.	*I admire Oliver Cromwell.*
The Famine? Well, you have to laff, now.	*The Potato Famine was a hilarious episode.*
Irish doos be a did lengwidge, altogither.	*Gaelic is a dead language.*
Them Provoes is morderin swine.	*The Provisional IRA are psychopathic scum.*
Them Provoes is sound out.	*The Provisional IRA is a force for good.*
Fairmers gits toe mooch.	*Farm incomes are ridiculously high.*
Deary fairms is owd het.	*Dairy farming is a thing of the past.*
The I.D.Air is a browtle ripoff.	*The Irish Development Agency is a milch cow for con men.*
Ile? There doos bi no ile in the Celtic Sea.	*There is no oil within 500 miles of Ireland.*
Didja hear anny good wans in the box toda, Faither?	*Hear any juicy ones in the confessional this morning, Father?*
Knack is what you'd call supersteetious.	*The shrine of Knock is the greatest magic lantern show on Earth.*
Peckit a Durex, ta.	*Packet of Durex, please.*

General

It's me helt, dacter.	*My health is not what it might be.*
What is it, now?	*What seems to be the trouble?*
It's them elliptical fits.	*Epileptic fits.*
It's that Dootch ellum disease.	*Dutch elm disease.*
I am destroyed wit spots.	*General spottiness.*
Me nerves is at me.	*Irritability, nervousness.*
Would yez tek the rats off the walls for the Da?	*Could you come and soothe my father's Delirium Tremens?*
He's on the bed wit a year.	*He has been in bed for a year now.*

Hev you seen himself?	*Have you seen the master of the house?*
Above in the attic.	*In the attic.*
Inside in the bear.	*In the bar.*
Beyond in the jacks.	*In the toilet.*
Below in the tome.	*In the grave.*
Massive!	*Splendid!*
Only massive!	*Absolutely splendid!*
Didla!	*Awful!*
Disprit!	*Frightful!*

The North

Hay dags wath the rang fat.	*He is a Protestant.*
Hay dags with the rang fat.	*He is a Catholic.*
Ae lav dane the Sharnkle.	*I am a Protestant.*
Ae lav dane Davas Flarts.	*I am a Catholic.*
Ae lav an Landandarra.	*I am a Protestant.*

Ae lav an Darra.	*I am a Catholic.*
Hears the lards.	*Here are the UVF, IRA, UDA, INLA, etc.*
Ean Peasla's arrate.	*I am a Protestant.*
Jarra Ardam's arrate.	*I am a Catholic.*

Nee parkin.	*Danger! Car-destroying robots.*
Nee peean an funna munna.	*We do not accept Irish Punts.*

Et's all varra sard.	*It is a tragedy.*
Et es.	*Yes.*
War all hayman.	*We are all people.*
Way air.	*Yes.*
Will, now.	*So why can't we live in peace?*
Nee sarranda.	*No surrender.*
Nee calanillism.	*No colonialism.*
Oytsade, yu.	*Would you come for a short walk?*

Armageddon Wet

Tes a bed dee.	*A depression is approaching from the Atlantic.*
Tes a bed dee so. Bad wether.	*While you were speaking, the wind has commenced lashing in from the South West bearing rain in vast quantities.*
Ah, tes a bed dee.	*Yes. The wind is now shrieking from the West. The rain is horizontal, and the mountains are obscured by a low grey roof of cloud.*

Raight, so. Bed wether.	*Waves are breaking in the market squares of West Coast towns as the wind backs northwesterly. Every lifeboat in Ireland is out. Inland, rivers have burst their banks.*
Tes a bed dee, raight enoof.	*A ridge of high pressure ten minutes wide has just flashed across the country, bringing with it thick fog. A nuclear aircraft carrier has collided with a Celtic Sea oilrig and is falling victim to the China Syndrome.*
Ah, tes a bed dee, so.	*The wind has turned southwest again, carrying clouds of radioactive mist across the Central Plain. Cattle and humans are dying like flies.*
A bed dee, all raight.	*A giant crack has opened across the centre of Ireland; great geysers hiss volcanic steam into the overcast. Winged demons flutter out by the millions.*
Bed wether.	*It has commenced raining blood and frogs. Giant bats wheel among the gale-lashed towers of what was once Dublin. A fell beast slouches towards Bethlehem to be born.*
Will we go te Meunis?	*Shall we have a drink at Mooney's bar?*

Festivities at Home

God bliss all here.	*Evening, all!*
Sorry for your trooble, missis.	*My deepest and most heartfelt sympathies.*
You'll hev a bottle.	*Some beer?*
You'll tek a lairge bottle.	*A pint of beer?*
You'll tek a dhrop.	*A full tumbler of whiskey?*
There, now.	*I will watch as you drink it.*
Will ye come and see the da?	*Come and visit father.*
I will.	*Yes, willingly.*
He is inside in the end room.	*He is in the parlour.*
Doon't he look loovleh?	*He makes a most attractive corpsh.*
He do.	*Quite true.*
Ye have a grand dea for it.	*Eshlent weather for funerals.*
We have.	*Quite true.*
Hi look so payceful, like.	*He looksh sho . . . well, dead.*
Sure tis the end of us all.	*It will come to all of us, some day.*
Wad ye come to the kitchen, now.	*Come and blot up the whiskey with ham.*
Jasus Murphy! Toe leet!	*Our honoured guest has measured his length beside the corpse.*

Jeames is gittin wid.	*James is getting married.*
The feather is efter findin him inside in the ditch wit a wan.	*The priest discovered him. in the hedge with a girl.*
The feather hunted him out of it.	*The priest chased him out of it.*
O, he's a heppy men arright.	*The priest is delighted.*

Tes a gorl!	*It's a girl!*
God loovus, that makes elevin.	*Oh, no! That makes eleven!*
Bitter look next time, missis.	*Don't worry, wife! We'll knock a son out of you yet!*

Artificial Irish

Top of the morning, Paddy!	*Good morning. I am a tourist.*
You're a fine broth of a boy!	*You, on the other hand, are not.*
Not like that spalpeen Mick!	*I do not like your brother who lives close to me in Highgate (Brooklyn).*
Yer sister, now. There's a colleen!	*Your sister has a certain rude charm.*
I wouldn't be after dhrivin her away.	*Nudge, nudge, if you take my meaning.*
No, begorrah!	*Er, yes.*
She's loike Kathleen Mavoureen.	*She has raven hair, pale skin . . .*
Her oys are smoilin . . .	*and eyes . . .*
loyke the oys of Varl Doonican.	*like Paddy McGinty's goat's.*
Arrah, bejabers, yis.	*Er, don't you think?*
Paddy, ye're a gintleman.	*Paddy, you have not hit me yet despite appalling provocation.*
Point a Liffey wather for moy man!	*A pint of Guinness and a Cherry B. for me, please.*

Arrah Kattleen the moan is waypin.	*I am on stage dressed in a long skirt.*
O the shwans the shwans.	*I am tearing my white locks.*
The crowel shwans.	*I am weeping passionately.*
Wadye not have spared me the shwans . . .	*I am grovelling, stage . . .*

Bejabers?	*. . . right.*
Curtain.	*The last member of the Abbey Theatre audience has just left.*

Getting on in the Literary World

Paint a stoat.	*Pint of Guinness, please.*
A was on the Narth Circular wit Behing.	*I was a friend of Brendan Behan's.*
Jasus we hed soom jairs.	*We used to get drunk together.*
A was in Peris with Jayce.	*James Joyce and I were pals.*
Ha wroot the Weak for the Americans, did you know that?	*'Finnegans Wake' is a commercial novel.*
And owd Yeets.	*I also knew W. B. Yeats.*
I planted some beanrows for Yeets, Nine, there was.	*I did some gardening for him in Innisfree.*
Till a met Heaney he never wrote a thing.	*Seamus Heaney is another pal.*
Well some dorty limericks, ye know.	*I turned him from dirty limericks to poetry.*
And Idmund Spenser.	*Also Edmund Spenser.*
The Faery Queen was about poofs, till a cheanged it.	*'The Faerie Queene' was about a gay bar in Thurles till I rewrote it.*
I'm a bit of a man for the music, too.	*I am also deeply musical.*
A tot the Chieftains to plea.	*I taught the Chieftains to play.*
And Vanmarson was deliverin wan a found him.	*And Van Morrison was a delivery boy when I discovered him.*
Ball o' malt, thankye.	*Large whiskey, please.*

Emergency Irish

Cowrig lyum!	*Help!*
Mi fayther lyum chach air na chuffer.	*I have lost my legs.*
Chicher shlee chan na fariger?	*Which way to the shore?*
Thaw ma chaid aregid air fahd egg na yowl lak adoori.	*The bookies have got my money.*
Thawn culture sa keogh.	*I am lost in the fog.*
Co will an chach carna?	*Where is the pub?*
Co will an chach na nassal?	*Where is the toilet?*

APPENDIX

Stock Driving Calls

LANES CLOGGED BY agricultural livestock are a constant hazard to the regional traveller. In former times, there were specific regional driving calls for each type of animal. Improved breeds have broken up the region-specificity of the calls. But if you run through all the calls below, you will find that one works better than the rest. Stick with it. Advanced students will be able to tell the difference between e.g. a sheep and a pig and will thus save themselves some throat-wear.

Cattle: Coop! Hoaf! Mully! Proo! Proochy! Prut! Werp! Girp an Laydun!
Calves: Moddie! Mog, mog, mog! Pui-ho!
Sheep: Co-hobe! Ovey!
Pigs: Check-check! Cheat! Dack-dack! Giss! Lix! Ric-sic!
Turkeys: Cobbler! Peet! Pen!
Geese: Gag-gag! Fy-laig! Ob-ee! White-hoddy!
Ducks: Bid, bid, bid! Diddle! Dill-dill! Wid! Wheetie!
Pigeons: Pees! Pod!
Rabbits: Map!